"ENGLISH ONLY ENGLISH"

OUR LOST MALAYSIAN HERITAGE

Craig Iley

Copyright © 2023 Craig Iley

All rights reserved

No part of this book may be reproduced, or stored in a retrieval system, or transmitted in any form or by any means, electronic, mechanical, photocopying, recording, or otherwise, without express written permission of the publisher.

ISBN-13: 9798395386861
ISBN-10: 1477123456

Cover design by: Art Painter
Library of Congress Control Number: 2018675309
Printed in the United States of America

For our parents, Alf & Maureen, and 'Lily' & Joe.

With love and heartfelt thanks for all they have given and continue to give us both.

And for the friends, those we know and those we have yet to meet, who willingly offer a helping hand on this shared journey we call life.

For Alastair,

A very good friend indeed.

Best Wishes

Craig

PREFACE

There is an old expression, that says "when life gives you lemons, make lemonade".

Well, life has just turned up with a very large bag of lemons. A big enough bag in fact, to make sufficient lemonade to give me diabetes.

Well bugger that! I have no desire to dive into a sugar induced death spiral so I decided to re write it.

"When life gives you lemons, go on a road trip. Ask the universe what the hell is going on, and see if you get any anwers."

Amazingly it worked!

PROLOGUE

Looking back on it I suppose the journey to Malaysia actually began on the A19 when I was travelling up to Washington to meet my friend Chris. It was October 17th, a beautiful bright, sunny, morning.

Although I am usually very conscious of the passing of time, 2022 was a year I would be very grateful to see the back of and I suspect many other people were feeling the same at that point, particularly anyone in the business community.

The year had in fairness, begun with some considerable promise. The situation with Brexit was beginning to settle down, my various projects were on track.

We had recently secured investment including a very high-profile international backer for our business and everyone was looking forward to the ending of Covid restrictions, something which brought with it the promise of life returning to a normality that had not been seen since 2019.

That promise lasted until exactly February 20th when our Russian friends decided to invade Ukraine. We had watched as the rhetoric and tensions had slowly built over recent months, but if we were honest, we had taken our eyes of the ball. All most of us were really concerned about was the pandemic.

I don't think many people really believed we could be

facing another war in mainland Europe with a major power. Yes, we had weathered a regional problem in the Balkans in the 1990's, but the prospect of a face-off with Russia was quite another order of magnitude altogether.

When major events like this happen, they don't tend to happen in isolation and surely enough in this case, the events playing out in Ukraine were producing what can only be described as a series of very unfortunate events here at home.

In short, the narrative ran something like this.

The war broke out, immediately resulting in western sanctions, which in turn led to the cutting off of the gas supply from Russia, which then resulted in a massive spike in inflation and a cost-of-living crisis.

Major stock markets had their worst six months since 1973. US tech stocks in particular were hit, the five biggest stocks alone lost over one trillion dollars in value, and the capital markets took flight.

As we entered the second half of the year the picture brightened slightly but it was short lived and, by the end of September the markets were testing new lows.

To complicate matters further there was a change of prime minister, Boris Johnson got his marching orders and Liz Truss stepped up to save us all.

Well it couldn't get any worse could it? Oh, hang on a minute, apparently it could, and it did, when she decided to hastily introduce a set of badly thought through economic policies which succeeded in spooking the markets even further.

The pound plummeted on the money markets, forty percent of lending products were withdrawn from the market in a single day. Commercial lending stalled overnight, interest rates started going through the roof, pension funds were reeling from the unwinding of their borrowing led investment positions leaving us all worse off, and investors were fleeing for the hills.

It's not too much of a stretch to say, "the shit was hitting the fan big time." Watching this unfold was like a waking nightmare and knowing how serious the ramifications would be I was feeling punch drunk. Although all of these things are outside of my control, I felt like I had a touch of the negative Midas syndrome.

All I was waiting for was for Morgan Freeman to be elected President of the USA, take over my television set, then tell me there was a comet on its way.

Of course there was, why wouldn't there be?

In all my years in business I have never known a year like it and, truth be told I was at a very low point. I was feeling like a plank of wood that had been stretched across a barrel and people were gradually adding weights to each end. How long would it be before I snapped, I wondered?

Everyone deals with stress differently but for me this introspection, these thoughts of self-pity are too alien, they are too self-indulgent. It's nothing personal, hard times are looming large on the horizon for everyone.

Even as I become aware of these feelings as they rise and fall within me, I know that there are a lot worse things going on in the world, that I have much to be grateful for. Even so, I am only human and I know that I need help to find a way through this. Where could I turn?

Maybe what I really needed was a chat with an understanding friend to help me regain a sense of perspective.

With that firmly in mind I rocked up at Chris's house, had a coffee while he finished his cigarette outside in the garden then we took his dog, Jake, for a walk along the river and had lunch in a pub a few hours later.

Well, what are you going to do?" he asked.

"I have some things to work through that will take until the year end at least" I said, "but honestly I suppose what I really need is to take some time out."

I had always promised myself that when I finally finished work, I would take a long trip."I think I will head to the far East for a month in the New Year.

"Good "he said. "You need some time away to re-evaluate, to process what has happened and maybe a month isn't going to be long enough."

He was probably right but that was all I could do for the foreseeable future.

I am in no doubt that I am looking at the end of my working life in and my feelings catch me off guard a little. Retiring is something that I always thought I would look forward to, but when it comes so abruptly it is proving to be something of a shock.

I was not exactly easing into it and the stress was also taking its toll at home, so that evening I suggested to my wife Sue that we head to South East Asia and we began making plans.

I soon discovered, that when you need to make a plan, that there is nothing worse than staring at a blank piece of paper, so I stop waiting for divine inspiration and grab an old Atlas from the study.

We eventually settled on Malaysia, and after a week or so an itinerary starts to take shape which allows us to set about completing the jigsaw of flights and accommodation, one piece at a time, until at last I could see some light at the end of the tunnel.

Although I don't know it yet, we are about to meet some remarkable people who will help us gain a greater understanding of our family roots, and the universe is about to show me that nothing happens by accident.

CONTENTS

1. The Road to Malaysia : A Quest for Truth
2. Singapore
3. Raffles & The Empire
4. Little India & Chinatown
5. Fullerton No! 'Grab' maybe?
6. Sweeping Up
7. Johor Bahru
8. First Impressions are better second time around
9. You say Melaka, I say Malacca
10. A River or a Canal?
11. A fellow Pilgrim
12. Kuala Lumpur
13. The Batu Caves
14. Down to Earth with a bump
15. Nev's new blowpipe
16. An England Long forgotten
17. Tanah Rata Bingo
18. Snotty Eggs and Road warriors
19. Georgetown
20. Penang Hill
21. Kek Lok Si Temple
22. Babas and Nyonyas
23. From the Boro to Batu Ferringhi
24. St Xavier's
25. The Clan Jetties
26. January 31st, 1926
27. Ipoh – Part 2

28. The road to Pangkor Laut
29. Paradise Found
30. "They're good on a barbecue"
31. "His name is Kevin"
32. Colonel what's his name?
33. Final words

THE ROAD TO MALAYSIA : A QUEST FOR TRUTH

In the end, Malaysia wasn't just a random choice of destination, there was another reason for heading there.

There was something else we had been putting off for a long time, something that would hopefully take my mind off things at home for a short while at least, and would provide answers to some very personal questions for Sue.

Sue was born in Bukit Besi, a small settlement near the town of Kuala Dungun, in the state of Terengganu in what was then Malaya, to a Chinese mother and English father.

She spent her early years there but has been in England since the 1970's. Sadly her parents are no longer with us and, as one does, she had fond, but in many cases vague, memories of her early years in Malaya.

Her mother rarely spoke of her home, she herself never returned so as a result, there was much Sue did not know of her Chinese - Malay Heritage.

They say you never really know your parents as people, which is strange as, if we are lucky, we spend the greater part of our lives with them. Now we are older and parents ourselves we can see it from the other side too and I guess it's not that much of a surprise when you think about it.

As parents you are meant to be the solid foundation that your children build their lives around. You are meant to be strong, to be reliable, always right, to always encourage, to nurture them, to protect them and to pick them up when they fall.

You are not supposed to be human, every bit as frail, frightened or unsure of life as they are, even if that is the truth which we hide from them. We are every bit as subject to the vagaries of fate.

A realisation dawns on us that the odds that have resulted in where each of us finds ourselves today, are literally billions to one. This is true for every one of us, but none more so than for those of mixed heritage.

I asked her, "what do you know about your parents, of their early lives and of their experiences in Malaya?"

Together, diving head long into the past, gradually we peeled back the layers from a very few, scattered family memories.

Slowly, a picture of a very different world began to emerge, one long since gone but one which never the less, still casts a very long shadow.

Set in the days of The British Empire, it was a world between wars, when the faint afterglow of Queen Victoria still held sway in terms of how one should behave.

Radio and powered flight were relatively new

inventions, women in the UK were neither allowed to vote, nor were they allowed to hold and dispose of property on the same terms as men.

It was also a world of great social upheaval, rapid change, and great opportunity for the adventurous. This is the world our parents were all born into.

Joseph Henry Stirland was born in Middlesbrough on September 10th, 1925, the eldest of eight children. After his national service he left England as soon as he was able, working in the Palestine Police Force until the settlement of 1948, when he left for a post in the Royal Malayan Police force.

Hor Yook Lin, 'Lily' was born half a world away on January 31st, 1926, in the town of Ipoh in the state of Perak in Northern Malaya, the eldest of four children. She had two brothers, Kim Seng, and Yik, and a sister known to us only as 'auntie baby'.

Lily was sent away not long after her birth to live with and in effect to be raised by, her grandparents on the island of Penang, more specifically in and around the Chulia Street and Campbell Street area of Georgetown. When she did eventually return to the family home in Ipoh, her mother and father were in reality strangers to her.

We had so many unanswered questions. Why would you send a new born infant away? Boys have always been highly valued in the Chinese culture, was it because she was a girl, or was it simple economic necessity?

As soon as she was old enough, she returned to Penang to train as a nurse. By a simple twist of fate,

Lily and Joe met when he took an injured colleague to the hospital and the rest as they say, is history.

They married on May 16th, 1953.

Their three children Peter, Anne, and Susan (Sue) were born in 1954, 1958 and 1963. Until 1969 Lily and Joe would have been considered to be living a very privileged life.

Peter was privately educated in boarding schools, first in Penang, then in England, whilst Anne and Sue attended a convent school. The family lived in relative luxury, they enjoyed good quality accommodation and their lives were made easier with the help of servants but regular moves within the country were necessary.

They lived in several places, the locations driven by Joe's need to work, but the last place, and perhaps naturally the one that stuck in the memory of a seven-year-old girl is Seventh Mile, in the town of Batu Gajah just outside Ipoh.

Although they wanted to stay in what had become the Federated States of Malaysia, by 1970 the world and their situation was very different making this impossible so they had to make a difficult choice. The decision was eventually taken to return to Middlesbrough where they settled down to a new, very different life.

For Joe this was no longer the place he had left in the 1940's, but at least much would have been familiar, including the local shipyards where he found work. Not so for Lily however, for her this new life must have seemed very alien, cold, and uncomfortable.

Why had they chosen to come back to the UK? and when they did, if any of the children spoke Malay or Cantonese, why had Lily been insistent that the children left behind their Malay heritage with her mantra '**English, only English!**'

By the time our plans were made this trip would become something of a pilgrimage for both of us. She in search of her past and her parents, and me in search of some inner peace.

Peace however was going to take some time to arrive.

Our itinerary is not complete, some travel arrangements could not be made as we would have wished but we thought 'how hard can it be?" and our intention was to fill in the gaps after arriving in Southeast Asia.

The first problem was that we would not be able to visit Terengganu on the East coast after all as it was still the monsoon season there.

When you look at Malaysia on a map, excluding the islands on the East in the South China sea such as Borneo, the peninsula looks like a long thin strip of land that stretches from Singapore in the south, running up to Thailand in the North, but this is an oversimplification.

It is something of a surprise to find that the climate on the East and the West coast can be so different. The southwest monsoon season which affects the west coast occurs from late May to September.

The Northeast monsoon season which affects the East coast, lasts from November through February. Helping to maintain the distinct weather patterns is a long, and deceptively high mountain range which runs down the centre of the peninsula; but more about those later.

Sue consoles herself with the fact that much of the family history she wanted to explore was centred on the areas around Penang and Ipoh, so for now we would be going to Singapore.

From there we would cross over the border and make our way up the West Coast of Malaysia, visiting

Johor Bahru, Melaka, Kuala Lumpur, The Cameron Highlands, Penang, Ipoh and Pangkor Laut.

So far so good!

SINGAPORE

As if testing my resolve to find a new perspective, fate gives me one last little lemon flavoured prick, just in case I want to change my mind about making lemonade.

When the time comes around, my kitchen ceiling is about to fall through from the leak in the shower upstairs.

The plumber is three thousand miles away in Cape Verde and communications were not going to be easy while we are away, not least because of the eight-hour time difference so the best we can do is organise a sticking plaster solution until we get back.

On January twelfth we say goodbye to our daughter Elizabeth and our son Josh drops us off at Newcastle airport for the flight to Dubai. It is cold outside and I for one am looking forward to the promise of warmer weather.

As I stand shivering in the car park, I can't help feeling that I may have jumped the gun a little, being dressed in only a shirt and jeans. Partings like this are always bittersweet moments. It is sad to see Josh go because we won't see him again until Easter as he has his own quest awaiting him, so for now we are heading in opposite directions.

I would like to say that the airport understands this and does everything possible to make these moments special for all their travellers but they don't. They have all been to the Dick Turpin travel academy, so he also needs to get out of the car park soon otherwise he will need to apply for a mortgage to pay the exit fee.

Ahead of us is an eighteen-hour journey with a short layover in Dubai so, as his tail lights disappear into the distance, we head inside where we do what all holidaying couples do. We realise what we have forgotten to pack and argue about whose fault it is. Oh how we laughed.

The flight on the Boeing 777 wide bodied jet is comfortable, smooth and the service is good. We are heading East, away from the setting sun so as we approach Dubai only seven hours or so after take-off, it is already dark.

It is not a bad introduction though, it is actually quite poetic, everything you would expect of the Middle East. We can see the bright lights of the city lit up under the horns of the crescent shaped moon, set in the clear night sky.

I have always felt that air travel is a very brutal way to get to one's destination. Obviously for most people it is the only viable option for international travel but I have often envied those travellers in centuries past who would have taken weeks on their journey.

They had time to acclimatise, time to really take note of the changes in the weather and the culture in the exotic lands through which they made their way.

Alas the poetry soon dissipates. There are no magic flying carpets, no thousand and one nights or Arabian adventures here. It is obvious even from twenty thousand feet that Dubai is all about bling and glitz and the airport terminal is the same.

On the plus side it is clean, it's also full of top-of-the-line designer shops, but to be honest it could be an airport anywhere; Heathrow, New York, or Miami, are not so different.

As we are simply transiting rather than leaving the airport the only real give away that you are in the Middle East at all is the duty-free shop, where a huge golden camel seems to welcome you in to sample multiple types of dates or figs that most Europeans don't even know exist. It is a pleasant enough place to kill a couple of hours until it is time to board the flight to Singapore.

Mission accomplished, a few hours later I am about to see the other face of modern-day travel and what a miracle it is. On the way down the air bridge, I notice people stopping, they are looking out of the windows and taking pictures. When I finally reach the aeroplane, I suddenly realise why they were so transfixed.

We are about to board an A380 Airbus, the largest commercial airliner in history. It has two floors, can accommodate around eight hundred passengers and crew plus their luggage. It is a truly astonishing machine that makes a Jumbo jet look like a mid-sized saloon compared to a Humvee.

For anyone who is not regularly immersed in the world of aviation or who is not an aeronautical engineer, the idea that this behemoth, fully loaded weighing one and a quarter **million** pounds can not only fly but can fly at over six hundred miles an hour for over eight thousand nautical miles is a mind-boggling affront to the senses.

The flight itself is fortunately uneventful. We arrive in Singapore early on Friday morning, collecting our luggage before jumping into a taxi to take us to the Pan Pacific Hotel. We are in need of a shower and a few hours rest and fortunately a room is ready for us upon our arrival.

The room is rather nice. It has floor to ceiling windows complete with electric blinds and surprisingly there is also a large bath, which I soon discover with the right configuration of blinds, can be used whilst looking out over the city scape.

Whilst I soak in the bath the weariness of the journey quickly begins to fade and I turn my attention to the practicalities of our trip. The hotel is having quite a lot of work undertaken in the common areas. We were not told about this at the time of booking, which was naughty, but fortunately it is not intrusive.

I remind myself that it is OK to relax, I am in search of a more positive perspective. With the approaching weekend the work will cease for most of our stay here.

Singapore and Malaysia sit very close to the equator which means that there are roughly twelve hours of daylight every day. This is very welcome having come from England and a cold dark January where the days are currently less than eight hours long. It also means that the temperature only varies from about 28 degrees at night to 32 degrees during the day and the humidity is typically around 90%.

The promise of sunshine and warmer weather is enticing but this will take some getting used to.

One strange thing about Singapore is that none of the UK phone providers appear to have any roaming agreements with counterparties here, so using the phones will be prohibitively expensive. Fortunately, we are only here a few days. Leaving them in airplane mode means that we can simply make use of the WIFI, which is thankfully everywhere.

As a stop gap, we can just use WhatsApp for phone calls. This is not going to be sustainable for a month-long road trip however, so we will need to make better arrangements soon, but for now this will suffice.

There are a few things on our 'to do and see' list here so I surf the internet to get my bearings and identify some landmarks. Of particular interest is The Raffles Hotel, which although we don't currently realise, is actually just visible from our hotel room.

Like most of South East Asia, Singapore is famous for its fast food, sold from what are called 'Hawker Stalls.' As they pay so much attention to detail here, it is not surprising to find that these stalls tend not be distributed at random, rather they are clustered together in what are known as Hawker Centres.

Although we are shattered, we decide to head out to one of them and try some of the local food. We pick one at random, the Maxwell centre on the edge of Chinatown and the concierge kindly orders us a taxi.

As we wander around the stalls, the pungent aromas in the air of unfamiliar and exotic spices sets the mouth watering, increasing our hunger pangs and bringing with it the promise of new culinary sensations.

It also sets the tone for the next month. 'Street food,' as it is euphemistically known is not something that I would usually indulge in. For me it just conjures up memories of hot dog and burger vans outside the football stadium on a Saturday afternoon that are guaranteed to give me indigestion and raise my cholesterol, but it is a key part of the culture here which I have come to immerse myself in, and Sue loves it.

Tonight the clear favourite, which also seems to be the most famous dish here, is Hainanese Chicken simply served with rice, but it is immediately disheartening to see that the queue for the stall selling it is huge. We're both too hungry and impatient, so we quickly settle on a couple of other dishes of Chinese and Indian origin, then scramble to secure one of the plastic tables and a couple of chairs as the place is heaving.

Sitting down we notice that there are rucksacks nearby which have been left unattended. It is making me uncomfortable but my suspicions fade a few minutes later when four young girls approach us, retrieve their belongings, then to our delight they sit down at our table and begin to chat with us.

Getting to know some of the people on this trip is going to be vital if we are to get some of the cultural context that we badly need to understand. It is only our first night and our education is beginning in earnest.

The girls tell us that they all work for large multinational firms based in the city centre. They are smartly dressed and clearly very intelligent, typical accountant or investment banking types, no doubt high end graduates fast tracked onto the management ladder.

This is soon confirmed when they tell us that their work is high pressured requiring long days which makes it difficult to find time to cook, so they eat at the Hawker centres which fortunately are also very good value.

Although it is Friday night, they won't be going out partying, they are off home. We asked if there was anything valuable in their bags and they said yes, purses, laptops, phones etc. When we expressed our surprise that they would leave them lying around they seemed non plussed. "Why not? Singapore is very safe."

After a while we finished our meal and said goodbye. I am not exactly sure what I have just eaten, but it was very tasty. With full bellies and our sense of adventure in full flow, we both feel ready to make our first tentative foray to the edge of China Town where we could see all of the red lanterns and decorations lining the streets in preparation for the Chinese New Year, which was about a week away.

It promised to be an exciting place to visit but not for tonight, so we head back to the Pan Pacific promising ourselves an early start the following day. Weaving our way through an unfamiliar city scape, it proves to be a long walk back to the hotel.

Before we reach our destination, we find ourselves on the seafront allowing us to take in the incredible views of the bay and its major attractions. The Merlion, The Fullerton Hotel, The Marina Bay Sands Hotel, (that three towered monolith that looks as though it is topped by an ocean liner gliding through the air), the Cloud Forest beyond, and our appetite is again whetted for further exploration.

It has been a long, exhausting day and the adrenaline we have been running on is finally beginning to fade. Back at the hotel my feet are sweaty and sore, but at least the exhaustion also brings with it the welcome promise of a good night sleep.

True to our word we are up early, going down for breakfast at six thirty. As one always does on the first day when the breakfast buffet is both huge and enticingly different, we spend a good couple of hours trying absolutely everything.

The breakfast was indeed magnificent. Noodle soups, pastries, curry, rice, dim sum, dahl, European cheeses, salads, nuts, yoghurts, egg, beans, hash browns, mushrooms, toast, fruit, and the list goes on. By the time we left we have both had a four-course meal and for a second day running I had already eaten something I could not identify.

There were however no ill effects and although strange to me, much of the food is familiar to Sue from her childhood. The culinary experience here is going to be one of the bedrocks of the journey we have come to enjoy, not just for its own sake, but also because it is a strong link for Sue in her personal quest.

Our first task this morning is to find The Raffles Hotel. We have of course booked afternoon tea, as one surely must when in Singapore. Since this must be done quite a long time in advance, we don't want to miss it so we have one last look at the maps on WIFI and head out.

If the worst comes to the worst, we can always get a cab but it can't be more than half a mile away as the crow flies. The problem is that Raffles is a low-rise building from the colonial days of Empire, one which from our perspective now seems to have been somehow lost within a modern world dominated by gargantuan skyscrapers.

At first glance modern Singapore seems to be somewhat soulless. It is an ultra-modern city. One of the few that can truly claim to be 'world class.' It is perhaps what London and New York once aspired to be, but Singapore has not degenerated as they have. It is very safe, spotlessly clean and its development is often credited to the vision of one man, Harry Lee Kuan Yew.

LKY as he is commonly referred to, was a lawyer, a politician, and a statesman. He had studied in England as well as Malaysia, served as the first prime minister of Singapore from 1959 to 1990 and although understandably he wanted to bring his own cultural values to the fore, he well understood the need to establish an open economy.

He understood that the economy would have to be

one built on international trade if he was going to achieve his goal to turn a small island country, with few natural resources, into a global powerhouse.

To say he succeeded would be something of an understatement. Until it was very recently overtaken by Shanghai, Singapore was the busiest container port in the Eastern hemisphere and every major international bank or professional services company now maintains offices here.

He was a very interesting character and if anyone is interested, he is well worth reading about.

Singapore is not soulless however. One must explore a little to find it, but as we have yet to discover, it has vibrant ethnic communities and somehow the relationship with its colonial past seems to sit quite lightly amongst the ultra-modern buildings.

Although the two periods seem at first antagonistic, incongruous even, they both add something to LKY's vision that has been manifested here.

One thing that Singapore does have in abundance is shopping malls. They are huge, well connected via internal walkways to the major hotels, including The Pan Pacific and one quickly sees why they are the preferred thoroughfares. They are air conditioned and the alternative of even a short walk in 32-degree heat for the un-acclimatized visitor is not an easy task.

However, this brings with it two new problems. The first one is that Sue is enthralled with them and the second is a much more practical issue in that when you are walking around them you cannot see outside which means that you quickly lose your sense of direction.

When it comes to the shopping, Sue is captivated and doesn't know where to look first. Fortunately, the promise of re-acquainting herself with her childhood food memories is too much, eventually allowing us to move on from the window shopping. She is soon taking videos of the participants in what appears to be a cooking class and then, joy of joys, she stumbles upon chefs preparing the holy grail of meals that is fresh dim sum.

This proves to be a bittersweet moment as she can't get close enough because of two hungry children who seem to have had the same idea. They are currently in her way with their faces pressed up against the glass and are showing no signs of moving.

Eventually my sore feet and the need for coffee overcomes my patience, I need to sit down. Fortunately, we recognise 'Coffee Smith' which proudly boasts that it is open 24 hours a day, which by implication means the centre too is open all night.

We sit down overlooking the escalators to take a break. I must confess that I hate shopping and consumerism in all its forms.

Like everyone else I am a hypocrite and take its convenience for granted but it seems to me to be a type of madness, a sickness of the modern world that far from serving us, is slowly strangling the planet. Although I'm happy to let Sue enjoy it all, I am in my own little world of dark, shopping hating thoughts.

A moment later, she jolts my attention and '1,2,3 I am

back in the room.' She has been looking at her phone for things to do and remarks absentmindedly that she does not fancy a visit to the zoo.

I look across the atrium to the escalators beyond with all of the people and I can't help feeling a sense of irony. I should probably keep this thought to myself, but if this is not a zoo, what is it?

We finish our coffee and head out again on our quest to find The Raffles Hotel. Even though we believe the target of our reconnaissance mission is relatively close by, it is not long before we are completely lost again leaving us with no choice other than to leave the shopping centre by the nearest exit which leaves us at the mercy of the heat as we try to re-acquaint ourselves with some local landmarks.

A couple of hours later we stumble across Raffles which, as it turns out, is only a nine-minute walk from our hotel.

RAFFLES & THE EMPIRE

A t first glance Raffles is quite an unassuming, distinctly colonial, low rise, white walled building with a red pan tiled roof.

Situated on the intersection of two main roads it has a small car park and gardens to the front.

It is synonymous with Singapore, British Rule, and the name of Sir Thomas Stamford Bingley Raffles, the first de-facto British Governor of Singapore. A man who can also lay claim to being one of its founding fathers, though in a vastly different era.

His name is so intertwined with Singapore that it can be found on everything including buildings, roads, hotels, educational establishments, metro stations and much more besides.

Yet strangely, in the case of Raffles hotel, first impressions can be deceptive as it is not really the product of British colonialism at all. It started life as a beach house and the first hotel was built on the site when it was leased to a Dr Emerson in 1878, at which time it was called Emerson's Hotel.

He was granted a ten-year lease but unfortunately, he passed away half-way through his tenure and for the next five years it became a simple boarding house run by the Raffles Educational Institution, the oldest school in the country.

When the lease expired in 1887 it was taken over by four enterprising Armenians, the Sarkies brothers, who renewed the lease and opened a ten-bedroom high end hotel which quickly gained a reputation for excellence. It was named in honour of Sir Thomas Raffles who by this time was already long dead having died in England more than fifty years earlier, in 1826.

It retains its high-end exclusive reputation but it is no longer a small boutique hotel, having been extended many times. The building itself is in fact enormous, extending back over one hundred metres, it now houses numerous bars, shops, bedrooms of course, and garden areas, much of which is open for non-staying visitors to enjoy.

We avail ourselves of the opportunity to wander through the cool shaded courtyards into the gardens to take some pictures.

The grounds are beautiful and well-kept as one would expect. They are dotted with palm trees, water fountains and exotic plants, at once pleasing to the eye, providing welcome shade, a gentle aroma in the nostrils and a calming soundtrack. This is completely at odds with the busy roads outside, not to mention the huge skyscrapers that loom over us, clearly visible beyond the red tiled roofline.

The dress code for our afternoon tea is smart casual and in our T Shirts and shorts we currently only partially fit that description, the casual part, so we head back to the hotel to change.

Due to the jet lag, it is still feels like the early hours to us, but rather than take a nap I make use of the hotel WIFI to try to figure out how the metro system works. Checking the routes for Little India and China Town, which we hope to visit this evening, will save time later. It seems quite straightforward and will no doubt be cheaper than taxis so it is worth the effort.

Pretty soon, freshened up, changed, and armed with a clear idea of where we need to go, we head back out to Raffles for afternoon tea in the Grand Entrance Hall. This time, much to my relief, we do in fact manage the walk in under ten minutes.

Our reservation is checked before we are whisked to a table for two in the rather opulent and pleasantly cool, grand lobby. Declining the offer of champagne, we are soon presented with a pot of indigenous tea from the Cameron highlands, scones with jam, and clotted cream.

This is followed by a beautiful three-tiered, silver stand, full of various delicately ornate cakes and small sandwiches, all of which may be refreshed on request. There is a gently playing soundtrack in the background, perhaps a piano, and we settle down to savour the experience.

On the one hand it is a lovely piece of theatre that I would recommend everyone try at least once.

As the gentle music plays, the belly becomes pleasantly full and with the constant fussing of people seeking to make you ever more comfortable, you find yourself imagining the days of empire and the quality of life that the British administrators must have enjoyed here. A quality of life beyond that which most could hope to equal, even by today's standards.

But on the other hand, I know that it is the romanticised view of a history that never really existed for most people and in the end, it is very much a tourist trap with a clever use of what is often underutilised space in a hotel.

We pay the bill, which by the time the service charge and taxes are added is over £130 then take the opportunity to wander around the hotel and private garden areas whilst we are able.

As we make our way past the grand staircase, we notice that there was what looked like a small young girl playing a giant harp.

I realise that what I had taken as a soundtrack from

a piano, was in fact entirely down to her incredible talent with this ancient instrument. She seemed so tiny, dwarfed by the huge harp, the staircase, and ornate furniture around her but her music expanded out in every direction to fill the enormous space.

From the moment we arrived all the people have been simply lovely, but I don't think I have yet seen a female over five feet tall. Indeed, I subsequently discover that five feet is the median height of all females in Malaysia.

Just outside the Grand Lobby there is the 'Writers Bar' and I fancy for a moment the idea of spending some serious time there. There seems to be a strong link between writers and bars but I scarcely drink and so I find myself wondering if I should give up writing…. or should I take up drinking more seriously?

Sue must know what I am thinking because she rouses me from my daydreaming and suggests that we head over to the long bar for a Singapore sling. This is stranger than one would imagine because she is completely allergic to alcohol but it seems that whilst in Raffles this is the other sacrosanct tradition.

When we arrive at said bar however, there is a very long queue to get in, and those coming out all seem to be licking their wounds from the heinous damage inflicted upon their credit cards, so we decide to come back another day.

LITTLE INDIA AND CHINATOWN

Singapore is not a cheap city, it's probably on a par with many European cities in cost terms, so jumping into a taxi every time we want to go somewhere is going to do our budget no favours.

It is not just the cost though, traveling like a local is one of the best ways to really to get to grips with a new place.

The day is not over and although the heat is draining, we want to make the most of our limited time here so we head back to the Pan Pacific. After freshening up, a quick shower and changing back into our casual clothes, as darkness begins to fall, we set out again in an attempt to negotiate the metro system for the first time and head for the nearby Esplanade station.

Like the rest of the city, the metro stations are modern, spotless, and very user friendly. I was a bit apprehensive about Covid restrictions as Singapore has been very strict for the last three years.

With China opening up, a huge surge of cases is currently being reported so I don't quite know what to expect next. We have seen some people wearing masks but so far it has been quite relaxed. The only place it is still mandatory to wear a mask at the moment, is on public transport so we put ours on and approach the ticket office.

The cashier tells us that it is card only, and it cost one Singapore dollar per journey (about 80p). I don't have any bankcards on me so I bought a ten-dollar MRT card, pressed it to the pad and stepped through the barrier. Quickly realising I could not use the same card twice; Sue then used the UK bank card that she was fortunately carrying, allowing her to step through behind me.

I had figured out that we needed to make our way to 'Dhoby Ghaut 'on the Circle line, where we would then have to change to the North East line. Once we found the North East line the rest should be quite straightforward, one direction for 'Chinatown' and the other direction for 'Little India'. We chose the latter.

Upon leaving the station at Little India there was an immediate difference in the atmosphere. At the food hall there are lots of people drinking alcohol and there is what I could best describe as a determined police presence. It isn't intimidating but there is clearly something going on and when we get outside into the street, we suddenly find ourselves in the middle of the Pongal.

This was our first taste of the Hindu culture which we would both come to really enjoy as our trip progressed. The Pongal is a southern Indian/Sri Lankan festival that lasts for several days. Hindus do not eat beef, but the cattle are often working animals and this seems to be the only day of the year that they get 'off,' which explains why we find several of them laid down in a huge makeshift tent in one of the streets.

As we continue to explore along the brightly decorated streets and narrow alleyways, Little India is a total assault on the senses, all of them at once.

The people are thronging everywhere. It is not just busy, it is very loud too, with the noise of the traffic, the voices, the Indian music mixing with the hot and humid evening air.

The market stalls are covered with garlands of flowers, every shade of red, yellow, and orange, hanging above pottery and religious idols.

There are strange fruits and vegetables on offer and the smell of exotic spices is everywhere around us. The hawker stalls here are bursting with food, much of which is unfamiliar to me but I recognise that the majority at least, is vegetarian.

It is all too much for Sue and she is feeling breathless and anxious so it is not long before we make our way back to the metro station.

We do not however head back to the hotel. It is still early so with Sue feeling a little better after a welcome break from the crowd, we continue on the North East line, past 'Dhoby Ghaut' then on to Chinatown.

This area is culturally more familiar to her and, after our first taste of Little India, by comparison it feels like it might be a somewhat less daunting prospect.

The lunar new year is approaching though which means that Chinatown is also busy. As we had noted the previous evening all of the streets were lined with lanterns and it is Saturday night, so there is a busy street market in progress.

In a few short hours we have seen the complete contrast that divides Indian and Chinese cultures. Each wonderful in their way, but despite the same colourful exuberance, they could not be more different.

The former seems to be completely chaotic, fatalistic, a whatever comes is the will of the gods attitude, whilst the other is very ordered, very business focussed yet both have "filled our eyes with sights" and our heads with memories of strange and exotic places.

It is quite late when we do finally arrive back at the hotel and we are both exhausted even though we should have been full of beans as our body clocks were still set for many hours earlier.

FULLERTON NO! 'GRAB' MAYBE?

For travel to be a real adventure you have to explore but let's be honest, when time is short and there is lot to pack in, it is very helpful to be able to walk in someone else's footsteps for a while.

It's also fun. Trip Advisor would go out of business if this wasn't the case and we would have nothing to laugh about later when we wonder what planet 'Sharon from Milton Keynes' was on when she complained that the excess of ginger in oriental food played havoc with her bunions or that her husband 'Trevor' was surprised to find that chillies are badly named and are in fact not cold after all.

We don't need trip advisor today. We have a friend, Karen, who lived in Singapore for a while and being a 'well to do sort' we had picked her brains on things worth experiencing whilst we were here.

Karen recommended Sunday Brunch at the Fullerton Bay Hotel. It would be anywhere between £80 and £110 a head depending on drinks, but as it came highly recommended, this was the second thing that we had pre-booked before leaving the UK.

There are worse places to wake up than Singapore when you have jet lag, never the less it was another early start. We were down for breakfast again at 6.30am but Sue was a little subdued. Just how subdued was apparent an hour later when we left the restaurant and I noted that we were already down to just three courses for breakfast. That didn't bode well.

Even though brunch was not booked until 1pm she was not feeling well enough to keep the appointment. Yesterday had been a full day and rather draining. Maybe we had just done too much in the heat and humidity so we decided to cancel and we just set out exploring again, this time heading in the general direction of the bay.

The Marina Bay Sands Hotel is a spectacular sight. There is no doubt that it is an incredible piece of architecture and that its location adds to the feeling of grandeur, but as a place to stay, it seems to be a little isolated, a little 'out on its own.'

It is however not just a hotel; it is a whole a complex. Despite it not being as central as one might imagine, there are plenty of things both within, and nearby worth having a look at, so it is well worth the walk over the helix bridge that links it to the mainland.

As its name suggests the bridge is built to look like the double helix of a DNA strand. The structure itself is another incredible piece of work in its own right, but it is almost lost amidst so many other sights, such as the Arts & Science Museum, the vast Marina Bay Sands shopping centre and of course the huge ocean liner 'floating' about our heads.

The Marina Bay shopping centre is huge, arcing around the bayfront and ranging over several floors. It is full of the usual high end designer stores with all of the luxury European or US brands present and much more besides but it is the lower ground floor that is calling us.

Walking in the heat and humidity has left us in need some refreshment. As luck would have it, on the lower ground floor is the food hall. A glorious hundred-metre-wide circle filled with kitchens, serving almost everything you could think of.

Food halls in UK shopping malls are the most dreadful of experiences, but here the experience and the quality of the food could not be more different.

It is Sunday however and lunchtime is fast approaching so it is insanely busy. There are lots of families out enjoying their weekend, all with the same idea as us. We have to wait patiently to get some drinks and then we are very lucky to nab a small table.

I am in no hurry to move on. It is fascinating to see all the people, to wonder where they are from and where they are going next. But I know it would be unfair to linger for too long.

We have almost finished our drinks and are feeling a little guilty as people are circling all around holding plates of food, looking for somewhere to sit. We motion to a couple of Chinese guys that they can share our table and they are immediately grateful. What I should have realised is that they are not alone. There are more of them coming so we quickly finish and leave the table to them.

Although we are trying to blend in, the profuse sweating in the heat, the white socks and equally white skin from a lack of sunshine having come from a cold UK winter clearly mark us out as tourists but these interlopers could not have been more friendly.

Nor could they be more apologetic, perhaps they have their own guilty feeling that they are somehow chasing us away.

Whilst standing up to leave Sue is eyeing up their lunch, remarking that it looks delicious. They ask if she would like to try it. I know that she desperately wants to, but with that famous English reserve, she instinctively refuses and although they are quite persistent, she manages to politely back away leaving them to enjoy their lunch.

We both know that this is the most will power she is ever likely to have when faced with the food here.

"What are you smiling at?" she asks.

"Nothing." I replied

"The Cloud Forest looks reasonably close by, it's just across the across the hotel walkway that links the shopping area with the MRT and the gardens are beyond. Should we make our way there next?"

Although we follow the signs, I think we must have somehow gotten lost, as we soon seem to be making our way over roof tops. The views are great but I haven't got a clue where we are. It is a relief when we do eventually step inside again, finally finding the high-level walkway that runs right through the inside of the hotel building. The views from there are also great unless you happen to have an aversion to heights.

Thinking we are back on track after our little detour I am looking forward to seeing the Forest but as we step out into the open air on the other side of the building it begins to rain.

We hastily step back inside and within minutes it is torrential, streaming down the curved towers of the hotel and we are suddenly surrounded by dozens of people who, like us were all caught in mid journey, in one direction or the other.

After about ten minutes the rain stops. Although the sky looks quite full, we are already becoming familiar with the weather patterns and the daily afternoon rain. In another twenty minute or so, you would not even know that it had rained, everything will be dry again but the evaporating moisture only serves to increase the humidity.

From the top of the hotel walkway, the container ships and the cruise liners in the harbour to the southeast are clearly visible. Ahead of us, we get the first close up glimpse of the rather alien looking 'trees' that can be seen for miles when they are lit up at night. Somehow even from here though, the route to the gardens below is not as direct as it first appears.

These 'trees' are artificial. They are actually designed as frames for the wildlife and the plants but they are spectacular, they look like nothing on earth. So strange and exotic are these gardens that part of the Avatar movie was filmed here and it became the forest of the alien world 'Pandora.'

It is only late afternoon but walking in the heat has again taken its toll. We are both exhausted so after just a couple of hours we make our way back to the Marina Bay MRT. From there we can head back to the shopping centre adjacent to the Pan Pacific and alight at the Promenade (not to be confused with the

Esplanade) station.

We have walked miles again today. My feet are now ripped to shreds with cuts and blisters. Stopping at the food court enroute for some wonton soup, sliced char sui pork on a bed of noodles takes up the last few hundred yards my feet have to offer, before we finally arrive back to our room to rest. By seven o'clock it's time to give our real world exploring a rest for today. We move instead to the virtual world of the internet and wonder what we can do tomorrow.

The slower evening also gives me a chance to start to consider the gaps we still have in our itinerary. Our next stop after Singapore will be Johor Bahru. It's not far away but it is technically a separate country and we have no idea how to get there. After that we will also have to get from there to Melaka and on to Kuala Lumpur in due course and we have no transport arranged for those journeys either.

I really would like to have travelled by train or local bus more but the distances between cities are further than I had envisioned With luggage, in this heat it might prove tricky but I decided to check out what options we might have. One big surprise to me is the poor railway connectivity in Malaysia. It seems that you can make these journeys by train, but not directly and it is not long before I give up as the logistics soon prove overwhelming.

When we only have a few days in some of these places, to take half a day to get there just does not seem practical so what to do? Whenever we need a taxi here the concierge very kindly orders one but occasionally a car has turned up and we have attempted to get in only to be told we cannot because it is a 'Grab Car.'

Intrigued, I set to work doing a bit research and soon discover that 'Grab' has an app so I download it and start to browse through it. At first glance it is obviously a ride calling service. I don't tend to use taxis at home but I assume it is like any other taxi firm's app or maybe an equivalent for Uber?

I don't need it just yet, the MRT is so easy here there is no need for anything else but that takes a weight off my mind. At least now I can concentrate on Singapore again while we are still here, and I file my new discovery away for now, resolving to figure it out properly over the next few days.

SWEEPING UP

It's another 6.30am start again and today is our last chance to see the things we have missed. My feet are a little better and things don't seem too bad with the benefit of an early night behind us.

I would still quite like to get out on the water both to get a different perspective of the city and its incredible architecture, as well as to get a little relief from the constant heat.

We have not really explored the old colonial centre of town yet. This area is really centred on the banks of the Singapore river, just a little inland from the Fullerton Hotel, which itself seems to stand guard over the entrance to the river mouth.

Clarke Quay, just one stop from 'Dhoby Ghaut' station in the direction of Chinatown on the Northeast line, seems like a good place to start today, so we set off after breakfast, happy with our brand new plan.

It is still quite early when we exit the MRT on to the river front. The bank curves to the right and we cannot see much in that direction but we can see some colourful buildings on the other side of the river. Just off to our left there are also what look to be, a number of tourist boats moored along the riverside.

These are the 'bum' boats we had heard about so we headed left up towards what were obviously once some warehouses and which now seem to be in the midst of a regeneration program.

It is rather quiet though. The boat trips have not started yet, but as we stand in front of a kiosk reading the flyers Sue notices something in the river. I assume it's just a fish jumping or maybe a rat, but walking a little further past the moored boats, we are surprised to see a family of otters playing on the steps beside us, completely unconcerned by their proximity to people. They are not shy, but are clearly wild although they do look very healthy and well fed.

It is lovely to watch them playing but after a while they have clearly had enough of performing for us.

Perhaps they have another performance elsewhere or maybe they have just had a better offer, but they head off through the gap between the shops and cafes towards the main road.

Curious, we follow them wondering why they are heading away from the river. It seems they are not; they are simply avoiding the territory of another family of otters a little further up and they re-enter the river via one of the many small culverts in the bank.

We cross over the river only to find that the shops and bars are all closed. The opening times seem to be co-ordinated with the boat trips which don't start for another few hours so rather than waste time, we decide to walk to Chinatown and explore the market stalls there for a while.

In Chinatown we happen upon a tailor's shop, and whilst I would love to have something bespoke made for me, as this our last day we simply don't have the time but the owners are curious and keen to talk. The lady who owns the place is second generation Singaporean but her family hail from India.

When I explained that we had been to 'little India' she started to tell us more of the festival and its significance and also about the Chinese New Year.

She said that years ago all of the Chinese businesses would have been closed for around three weeks but now the imperative to earn means the focus is very much on making money, particularly after three years of strict lockdown, no tourists, and rising prices.

It seems that even the Singaporeans are feeling the pinch, and this is a prosperous city.

Now holidays consist of a long four-day weekend and many Chinese people will be travelling to meet family they have not seen in a while. In fact, this is the first major holiday since lockdown that families have been allowed to spend together.

Saying goodbye, we head back towards the MRT making our way through the indoor market where we are overwhelmed with offers of acupuncture, massages and Chinese remedies for every illness known to man.

This is a fascinating little place with jewellery stalls, money changers, food stalls and even an old man sitting on the floor with his tools, making shoes by hand.

I would like to linger here but time is pressing now and we get back to Clarke Quay just in time for the first cruise along the river and out into the Bay.

The afternoon rain clouds are already threatening so we sit inside just in case, but we needn't have worried. The bum boat trip is lovely experience in a hand-crafted wooden boat. The friendly and well-informed guides point out all of the interesting features from the colonial past. Fort Canning, The Supreme Court, The Asian History Museum, Empress Lawns, The Parliament building, The Victoria concert hall, the tributes to Queen Elizabeth and more.

Eventually we pass out into the bay area to see the famous half lion half fish monument perhaps unsurprisingly called the 'Merlion.' It is widely used as the symbol of Singapore and its people. The fish represents its origin as a fishing village and the lion signifies its original name 'Kota Singa' or lion city.

Such is the importance of the symbol that it had originally stood further up the river but had been moved to this spot on a promontory of specially reclaimed land in front of the Fullerton Bay Hotel in 2002, all because the construction of the Esplanade bridge in 1997 had blocked the view of the statue from the bay.

Heading back inland up the river it is the left bank which really grabs our attention.

This section had gone unnoticed this morning due to the curve of the river. Now we could see that it was lined with bronze statues of children jumping into the water as they once would have done, and of Chinese traders or merchants depicted chatting or leading oxen powered carts, laden with goods to the market.

Then there are the colourful shop houses with restaurants below, which line the riverbank. Each vies in turn to be the highest, as this was the ultimate statement of wealth in the eighteenth century.

Immediately upon leaving the boat, we head back down here to explore but within minutes the heavens open and the rain is belting down so hard that the rain drops bounce a foot back up from the floor after they hit the pavement.

A few brave souls continue their walk but very quickly they all look like drowning rats.

When it clears up, we continue our walk along the river bank before crossing over. Making our way towards Queen Elizabeth walk, then through the park we soon realise that we are quite close to the war memorial, which means that Raffles is just out of sight on the other side of the small park.

It is Monday and with the rain, we may have more luck in visiting the long bar so we make our way there. This time there is no queue, although it is quite busy inside. Being able to just waltz right in and take two stools at what is indeed an aptly named, very long bar, makes for a much better experience.

As with our previous visit to Raffles it is very easy to get carried away with thoughts of an imaginary colonial life.

The bar is certainly evocative, well stocked with lots of British alcohol, especially whisky. It has a dark wooden ceiling with 'punkerwaller' style fans, a black and white floor, a cast iron spiral staircase that presumably leads somewhere but is cordoned off.

The staff are all attentive and dressed in white shirts with grey skirts or black trousers. We are offered an alcoholic drinks menu and politely decline. Sue orders a mocktail Singapore sling and I order a coke which comes to about £24. If we had been drinkers, two Singapore slings comes in considerably north of that.

All along the staircase I notice large hemp bags of roasted peanuts in their shells and we are soon presented with a small bag to enjoy with our drinks. It is a tradition here that one eats the peanuts, throws the shells on the floor, and crushes them underfoot.

This is so strange, anyway I mean what kind of lazy git can't just put the shells in a bowl or an ashtray instead of leaving them for some other poor bugger to sweep up after them? But here in particular, in a city so pristine, so obsessed with cleanliness and being tidy it's almost a rebellious act so abhorrent one cannot but help feel a sense of shame.

This though is one of the 'must do' things in Singapore and as I look around at my fellow criminals I notice the strangest thing. None of them actually look happy to be here, they are just finishing their drinks and ticking off a bucket list of things to do. It is a shame really because it is worth the experience.

It would be very easy to run up a substantial bill here and as I look along, I spot bar the barman preparing a yard of ale. Someone is going to regret that in the morning.

Having savoured to the last drop, including the ice cubes, the most expensive glass of coke I have ever had, we decide to head out just in time to see another very long queue forming outside.

It is time to head back to the hotel to freshen up because we have one more 'must see' sight before we leave. Tonight, we are heading for Satay Street.

During one of our earlier rambling walks through the city we had passed the Lau Pa Sat Hawker Centre and been enticed in to see the many satay stalls serving large fresh prawns and chicken skewers by the dozen.

Quickly cooked over blazing charcoal and served with a spicy dip and a little cucumber, this is so popular that in the evenings the road at the side of the centre is closed off to allow the tourists and many locals somewhere to sit and enjoy this local, but internationally famous delicacy.

Lau Pa Sat however is open twenty-four hours a day. We sit down at the plastic table and chairs, order twenty mixed satay skewers and two bottles of water. This is a fitting way to end our trip as the further north we head the more rustic and prevalent the street food will become.

Oh, what the hell, we probably have time to pop inside for a dessert before we head back.

JOHOR BAHRU

The distance from downtown Singapore to downtown Johor Bahru in Malaysia, is only about twenty miles; but the journey is far from simple.

If you don't have a car there are three ways you can make this journey. You can take a taxi, or the metro, which has approximately fifteen stops on three different lines, to Woodlands train station, and clear immigration there before getting on the train to cross the border.

Alternatively, you can go by bus, which is equally complicated, and finally there are some taxi drivers who are licenced for cross border travel and can take you from Ban San Street taxi terminal.

Despite my craving for adventure, today at least, I can't help feeling that taking the easy way would be the sensible thing to do, so option three it is then. We check out of the Pan Pacific, say goodbye to the concierge at the hotel, and ask them to order us a cab to the Ban San Street taxi stand.

Then it all gets a bit 'cloak and dagger,' a very strange experience indeed. On arriving at Ban San Street, the taxi driver introduces us to a suspicious looking gent who rather furtively asks if we want to cross the border for a good price.

"That depends, how much is it?" I ask. "And will there be snacks?"

"Seventy Singapore Dollars" he replied (about £40)

"No snacks" he added.

I pretend to think about it for a moment before nodding in general agreement. Then he points us in the direction of a small people carrier and begins to wander in the general direction with our luggage.

I wonder briefly if this is how they do it in Calais and if I am going to have to cross the water in the dead of night by dingy?

Fortunately for us we won't have to do that, but the driver does suggest that we all take a comfort break before heading off. I am little puzzled by this given the short distance but it is good advice. We leave the city and for a while the roads quieten down at least until we approach the Woodlands border checkpoint about twenty minutes later.

On the Singapore side the driver asks us for our passports. He hands them, along with his own over to the border guard and following a quick glance into the back of the vehicle in our direction, we are quickly waived through, lulling us into a false sense of security as to how smooth this journey would be.

We then head out onto the Johor Causeway and somehow are immediately in the middle of a four-lane traffic jam that looks like it goes on for about a mile to the border check point on the Johor Bahru side. It's about mid-day and despite the traffic on our side of the road, the southbound carriageway is strangely quiet, with nothing more than a few motorcycles evident.

Gradually inching forward seems to make each minute drag out in to its own tiny eternity. If you are on holiday that's fine, but for the driver time is money and he has over two years of lockdown to make up for.

Eventually, losing will to live, he jumps into the outside lane which is reserved for buses, coaches, and lorries, but which seems to have been making a bit more progress than our lane and after another hour or so we are at a checkpoint once again, handing over our documents before winding down the windows to let the border guards get a good look at us.

I am guessing they don't see too many westerners here as they ask us to open the suitcases for a quick rummage around. Satisfied that we are carrying only a mixture of dirty and clean clothes, and that we pose no danger to the sultanate, we are free to make our way to the Hotel SuaSana, a high rise building just on the outskirts of the central district.

There are uniformed guards stationed here too, in fact we have seen quite a few in front of the nearby hotels and buildings. Immediately the feeling here is very different.

Unfortunately, our room is not ready but we are able to leave our bags allowing us to head out to explore unencumbered. The receptionist suggests heading to the main shopping mall and I am bit confused at first. The SuaSana is adjacent to a shopping centre but apart from a few food outlets there does not seem to be anything in it.

As we wander to the other side, we see a guard on what turns out to be the front door. Clearly recognising a confused expression when he sees one, he points across the main road to a much larger mall on the other side.

As we walk through the mall, I notice the train station and taxi rank outside the rear windows, so I make a mental note of the location. If I can't figure out the Grab car scheme then I may need one or other of these in a few days.

The shopping mall is actually very large and although similar in style to those in Singapore, any resemblance from the high-rise buildings and shopping malls are fleeting, they are simply not quite at the same level. I must remember we are no longer in Singapore and we need to use Malaysian Ringgits here. It seems a little silly using a different currency twenty miles apart; but once the shopping begins the differences really come into focus.

We buy a shirt, three t shirts and a pair of ladies' shorts, all for the equivalent of £50. They are all good quality and the same purchase in Singapore would have been at least four times the price. It is no wonder the inhabitants of Johor Bahru are known as the exchange rate kings of Malaysia. There are money changing outlets literally on every street corner here.

There is also night market on tomorrow night and we have been told that the stalls there are even cheaper than the shops, but many of the goods are the same. Honestly, if you are visiting Johor Bahru, considering how expensive clothing is in the UK and how much you carry, there is no point bringing any clothes here. Take my advice, just come with an empty suitcase and what you are standing up in. You will save a small fortune.

During our wandering the food outlets here have not gone unnoticed and there are some lovely little bakeries. Mixed in amongst the familiar items like croissants, there are also pastries like nothing I have every tried. Shopping done it is time to find a restaurant and order the now obligatory dim sum, soup and various other dishes covered with the inevitable red chillies.

To my surprise I have been eating the chillies for nearly a week now and they are not having any adverse effects which I can only put down to eating in moderation, eating slowly, walking a lot, drinking plenty of water and the fact that I am not drinking alcohol. It's either that or a pure fluke.

Since we left Newcastle, our phones have been in airplane mode and we have relied on the excellent local WIFI connections but we know that as we venture further into the country this isn't going to cut it so buying some local SIM cards is now making its way to the top of the priority list.

There was no point doing it in Singapore as their carriers don't even seem to have reciprocal arrangements with Malaysia. Fortunately there is a mobile phone outlet opposite the restaurant offering two SIMS with unlimited calls & texts and 30Gb of data for one month for the equivalent of £10 each, an absolute bargain.

I have a dual SIM phone and Sue has brought an old iPhone so we are now feeling reconnected and much more comfortable. The first order of business is to send the folks at home our Malaysian numbers for emergencies but even switching SIMs, all of the installed apps still work as normal so it is not just cheap, it is really easy too.

Who doesn't love a bargain? To put it in context, O2 quoted us each £6 per day with a much smaller data allowance plus extra for calls and text. This would have worked out at around £300 for the month.

That has killed a few hours and has been useful too but now it's time to head back to the hotel where, to our frustration, our room is still not ready. Instead of retracing our steps to the shopping centre once more we head down the bank on the street that runs parallel to the high street for a change scenery.

Here the road and pavements are very rough so you have to be careful of the deep gutters where the unwary could easily break a leg and there, two doors down, we pass by the methadone dispensary for drug addicts.

This answered my earlier silent question about why there are so many uniformed security guards around. We are definitely 'not in Kansas anymore Dorothy'…….and the journey to get to know the real Malaysia beyond the tourist sights has truly begun.

Now, there are druggies all over the UK. Piccadilly in Manchester city centre for example looks like the epicentre of a zombie apocalypse most evenings but I suppose you could say that about many of our large towns or cities. Here however, this comes as a real shock as Malaysia is notoriously anti-drugs, and trafficking still carries the death penalty.

That is a fairly serious deterrent by any measure. Yet clearly for those who know about these sorts of things the borders here are more porous than the long lines of traffic would suggest and this was probably what the borders guards were looking for in our luggage earlier. For any substance users this would really not be a good place to visit but if you were caught, they could certainly cure your addiction problem...... permanently.

Further down the street we come across an Indian Temple and what is clearly their version of Little India. The district is quite small, centred around this modest temple complex. The temple itself is open so we wander into the courtyard but we are not suitably dressed to enter the shrine.

Although the officials inside are friendly, offering us additional garments to cover up, we politely refuse for now. All I can do is just stand and stare, gobsmacked at the iconography on display, the layers of colour and meaning in the building in front of me. It is hard to describe the feelings these places evoke. Not sad, quiet, or deathlike as our churches at home can often seem but joyous, full of life, overwhelmingly friendly and welcoming.

The day is wearing on now and the heat has taken its toll. Eventually our room is ready and we are pleasantly surprised at the space. It seems that this is in fact an apartment building and the top few floors are really the hotel which means we have a very spacious one-bedroom apartment.

On the next floor up there is a laundry, a gym, a café/restaurant, and a small rooftop pool. It's been another very long day on the back of a busy time in Singapore, so we decide to make the most of the apartment space and watch the large screen TV which fortunately offers a small, but adequate selection of free movies too.

Looking out from the thirty second floor the views from here are awesome, stretching all the way down the high street, across the causeway bridge to Singapore beyond.

As night falls the city below lights up and it reminds me of Dover. The huge, wired security fences along the road and the checkpoints are clearly visible and the flow of traffic is now somewhat different with cars heading back to Singapore whilst hordes of bicycles are now heading north.

Having experienced the price difference here it's no surprise that so many people come here to shop. Conversely though, the wages are far higher in Singapore and that is why there is a constant stream of motorcycles as people take advantage of the lower cost of living here but choose to work in Singapore.

Whilst that should be straightforward in the 21st Century, they can spend several hours a day on the road. One can't help feeling that the commute must be a miserable one.

Watching the news it is clear that this must be a very topical issue as they are now proposing the introduction of a single checkpoint much like the Dover - Calais idea. Singapore officials will man the booths in Johor Bahru and vice versa.

During our wandering in Singapore, we had often gone to down to the MRT station around lunchtime and it was not unusual to find large groups of people sitting on blankets on the floor, sharing food. In the UK this would have been an intimidating sight but there it instinctively felt like a part of the daily routine of life. These were presumably some of the army of daily migrant workers taking their break in the cool underground stations.

During the course of the evening, I have been getting a lot of notifications from my new 'Grab' app which I am staring to realise is much more than just a ride hailing service. It's also the local version of Deliveroo, Cineworld, Booking .com, and more besides all rolled in to one. I don't need any of these things right now, but I really do need to figure out how it works.

The private ride hailing service and taxis have a dynamic pricing system depending on the time of day and demand. There seems to be two ways to book a ride but I can't figure out the access to the demand flow to be able to pre order one and check the busy times. As far as I can tell, when we leave it should cost us about four hundred and fifty Ringgit (about £90) to get to our next stop Melaka which is about a hundred and forty miles away. That will have to do for now.

Oh joy! I have received a text from the SIM provider and to thank me for being a valued customer of almost one full day, they have given me a further 5GB of data free.

FIRST IMPRESSIONS ARE BETTER SECOND TIME AROUND

My body may be starting to adjust to the heat, humidity, and daily rhythm here, but my internal alarm clock seems to be firmly stuck on 'early.'

The following morning at 6.30am we head up to the restaurant to take a look at the breakfast options. There are a few things laid out but for the most part it is not buffet style here, the food is cooked to order.

It is a nice enough looking menu but I can't face Nasi Lemak, Fish noodle soup, Longton with spicy sambal, mee curry, prawn curry or congee, (which is a type of rice porridge) So, its coffee, fruit juice and toast this morning before setting out to find the 'heritage trail.'

We head out down the tree lined main street in the early morning sunshine. It is a lovely walk along the stream which runs parallel to the road. The stream itself is by turns, open then covered with glass then open again. Even the water seems to sparkle as if it too is enjoying the sunshine.

We pass little India and keep walking towards the waterfront then near the end of the road, head westwards where we eventually find the 'heritage trail.' Upon entering Jalan Tan Hiok Nee, we are greeted with the sight of a tree and red lantern lined street, complete with old traditional shop houses on either side.

It is really rather quaint here but first things first. Our primary mission is to find the Salahuddin bakery, which is one of the oldest bakeries in Johor Bahru. It is famous locally for its curry puff pasties and they are also on our 'to do' list. Paying due attention to the Heritage Trail is going to have to wait a little while longer.

Despite wandering along the whole length of the street the bakery's exact whereabouts remain elusive so we continue on towards a collection of large buildings and gardens that had been prominent landmarks from our apartment window.

At first glance this looked like the kind of old colonial era set up that may have once been a governor's residence or perhaps the buildings may have had some military use in bygone days. As we stand at the gate looking up the long shrub lined driveway, pristine lawns and flowerbeds wondering how to get in, a soldier approaches us on a quad bike and makes it clear that whatever it is, it is closed.

I ask the soldier what this place is and he tells us that it is in fact the botanical gardens. There are a few people milling around inside, but they are working here. It is not yet open to the public and won't be until next year. That is a shame because it looks magnificent and I still can't get the colonial images out of my head however, as some of those lawns look suspiciously shaped and appropriately cut for cricket.

We don't have long here so we turn back towards the heritage trail area to see the beautiful western entrance which is marked by bright red Chinese lanterns and an ornate grey concrete arch, with the inscription 'Laluan, Kerbudayaan Tan Hiok Nee.'

Disappointed not to have found the Salahuddin bakery earlier, we try again, eventually figuring out that it is on one of the streets running parallel, so another slight diversion to our course is required.

Even though we are now in the right street, it would still be quite easy to miss the bakery.

The front looks like a series of non-descript plywood and chicken wire boards. There is only a small green and cream coloured sign which is hard to see from any distance, but the give-away is the queue of local people beginning to form up outside This marks it out as something other than one of the small general stores that flank it.

It might look rough outside. Inside however, on pristine stainless steel trays there are row upon row of fresh baked bread, poppadum, cakes and about a dozen types of spicy samosas, pastries, and local snacks.

"Well, it would be rude not to, wouldn't it?"

So, twenty minutes later having finished an assortment of local snacks we need a coffee to wash it down and head back down to a nice little café we had passed earlier this morning.

The 'Dona Bakehouse Patisserie' seems suspiciously out of place here. `It looks like a traditional European coffee house that would be more at home in Vienna or Prague but there is always a twist here. Watching people eat, my tastebuds are now salivating, so as well as my coffee I have poached eggs on sourdough toast on a bed of mushroom and smashed avocado.

Considering the simplicity of the meal, I have never seen a more beautifully presented dish. It arrived complete with edible flowers, various bits of shaved greenery, crushed herbs, and seeds. The only thing which takes the edge of this culinary experience is being presented with a spoon for an eating implement which, I must admit does throw me a little bit.

On passing the coffee shop earlier on our first trip along the street, we had noticed a very long queue and a sign with the time of the next bake which is partially what attracted me to it. It's prominent modern shop front sets it apart from the shop houses adjacent to it, which are set back a little from the street so we had not taken much notice of them.

But as we leave, we notice that the shop house next door (when I say shop, it basically consists of a door, a serving hatch, and a wood store for the ovens), is in fact the 'Hiap Joo Bakery & Biscuit Factory.' This is what the bake sign timings related to. So here we are five minutes later making our way back along main street to the apartment for a cup of tea equipped with a packet of locally made biscuits.

As night falls it is still 28 degrees but it is less intense than the mid-day temperatures. We venture out again towards the heritage area, where we have been told that the night market should by now have been set up.

Like everywhere here, the place seems to be completely different at night, it seems to really come alive. The gold and money changing shops are all open, the night market is bustling and well worth a visit. I must confess I am all shopped out so it is a short visit but I am glad to have seen it.

I am pleased too, to get a final chance to see the worshippers streaming into the now brightly lit Hindu temple before heading back in to the cool of the shopping mall for yet more Dim Sum, prawn and pork dumplings for our last meal of the day.

We are up at 7.00AM the next morning, it is going to be another busy day. There is just time for a light breakfast and handling the formalities of an early check out. Keen to get on our way to our next city, it is sink or swim time with the Grab taxi app, but all does not go according to plan.

I had checked the prices again earlier that morning and they were little changed but by nine o'clock the roads are really busy and I am in for a nasty shock. The taxis are coming in cheaper than the private Grab rides so I book one then wait patiently for it to arrive. Ten minutes later the app tells me that the booking has been cancelled for no reason that is obvious to me, so I try again.

A few minutes later the taxi driver calls to check where we are going to. When I tell him Melaka, he too cancels the booking but at least he does take time to explain that the licenced taxis cannot go beyond the borders of Johor and that Melaka is to all intents and purposes a different state.

Oh Bugger! I then have no option but to try to get us a private ride, and the way these work is that the driver needs to accept the route along with the estimated price which can take a little while if they are on the road already, which by now most of them are.

The price is now almost double at seven hundred and seventy five Ringgit (£160) but a little more is added, fifty Ringgits (£10) if we want to use the toll roads which obviously we do given that Melaka is several hours away.

There seems little to be gained by spending our

precious time sitting in traffic. Although I don't know it yet, even in this I was wrong, later in our trip we would gain a lot by sitting in traffic.

Eventually we get a taker for our electronic SOS. A Driver called Ng calls us to let us know he is stopping for petrol and will be with us in about ten minutes. When you get used to it, the app is quite good as you can track the cars on your phone so we can see that he is indeed just around the corner at the petrol station. True to his word he appears outside the hotel a few minutes later.

Our car is a small orange coloured cross over. It is clean and comfortable and pretty soon we are on our way, which is a relief for logistical reasons, but surprisingly I am feeling rather sorry to be leaving Johor Bahru so quickly.

Our journey is now starting feel more 'real' thanks to our time here. It has been a very real contrast to the polished, clean, highly organised, and expensive Singapore, where everything is easy to get to, but it has its gems if you are prepared to scratch the surface and to work a little to find them.

There is clearly a lot of investment going on here and now that Malaysia is re-opening after three years of covid lockdown, it would be interesting to see how it develops.

With the scenery rushing by it is not easy, but we do try to take note of the sights along the roads as we head out of the city. Johor Bahru is actually much bigger and more sprawling than we had realised.

Then, as one does, we start the usual conversation

with the driver. "What time do you get off?"

No, not really, but we do ask him if the roads are always this busy.

He explains that yes, the journey is always busy but there is a four-day national holiday coming up for the New Year Celebrations, and since Chinese people have not been able to travel for the last three years, they are expecting that some two and half million journeys will be made through here next weekend alone.

Wow! Even if it weren't for the exorbitant hike in the taxi rates, I think secretly he is also glad to be heading out of town too, this is likely to be a six hour round trip and it will keep him busy for most of the day. I can't say I blame him; it looks like a real nightmare looming.

For us however, the journey itself is relatively uneventful. The toll roads are much like any other motorway except that they are lined variously with rain forests interspersed with Palm plantations. I am tired and keep dozing but as the journey progresses Northwards, the South bound traffic is really building up now. Surely our driver won't relish the return trip.

As it turns out most Malaysians are very pragmatic, they always have a solution for this sort of thing. He knows our destination well, and explains it is no problem for him. He actually originally hails from the Melaka area, so once he has dropped us off, he will visit his aunt and his sister (presumably not the same person), have some food, then drive back later when it will hopefully be quieter. As we will discover it is very common in Malaysia for families to span a number of cities.

On our approach to the outskirts Ng kindly starts to tell us a little of the history of Melaka and to point out some of its landmarks, such as the airport which is now little used as the runway is too short for modern international jetliners.

He says it is just used as a pilot training school now, and for light aircraft and recreational flying. I think about the behemoth we flew in on and as we drive parallel with the runway, I can fully understand the challenge.

Finally, around lunchtime Ng navigates his way the last few miles through the back streets and back-alley ways, passing intimate little Hindu temples and Mosques before somehow, we suddenly emerge into the narrow street of 'Jalan Tokong' in the old town, opposite a Chinese temple at our destination, the Liu Men hotel.

YOU SAY MELAKA, I SAY MALACCA.

The state of Malacca gives its name to the waterway that runs between Malaysia and Indonesia. These 'straits' are part of the Andaman Sea which runs up the west coast of the Malaysian peninsula.

It is here that you first really become acutely aware of the racial melting pot that this country truly is. You also first start to consciously notice the ethnic mix, the Chinese Influence in particular, which is getting stronger as we move North.

About twenty-five years ago my cousin and her husband lived here for a couple of years. Unfortunately, I never had the opportunity to visit them, but all of the family who did manage to visit spoke very highly of the place and its people. This was really the reason that we ended up in Johor Bahru and using taxis, taking the road north.

If we had not have been coming here, we would have probably flown from Singapore directly to our next stop Kuala Lumpur, but I am so glad we did not. Melaka / Malacca is a beautiful place filled with history and for the Renaissance Europeans it was one of the original maritime silk road cities of the orient. This is a must on any visit to Malaysia, especially if you are interested in history.

The city of Melaka is the state capital and like most cities was originally a fishing village 'Kota' Melaka. It is the oldest city on the straits and it has UNESCO world heritage status.

It is hard to say for certain how long the Europeans have been trading here but there are clearly influences from Portugal, Holland, and of course Great Britain. All mixing with the eastern influences from Indonesia, China, Southern India, and the Arab traders who helped spread the religion of Islam across the region.

All this the city proudly celebrates, but there was also a Japanese presence here during the second world war. Although not forgotten, this was a very dark period in its history when many of the residents, along with captured British POWs, were marched north to be used as slave labour on the notorious Burma death railway.

One of Sue's abiding memories of her mother Lily is of her dislike of the Japanese soldiers she had encountered. Lily had been a child during the occupation and the tales of their legendary cruelty are not exaggerated. Perhaps unsurprisingly this theme would crop up again, towards the end of our trip.

Melaka is once again the welcoming melting pot at the crossroads of the East and West and, from the moment you step through the door, the Liu Men Hotel is a haven. A cool oasis of quality and charm. We are greeted at reception by traditionally attired staff offering us cold towels, along with a delicious homemade beverage incorporating lemon grass, ginger, water, and a little cane sugar syrup.

As I sign the register our bags are taken away and, as the room is not quite ready the concierge invites us into the bar for complimentary tea and coffee.

A few moments later a gentleman approached us and introduced himself as Mr Izhar Ibrahim, the manager, to enquire if we need anything. He enquires about our trip and he could not have been more helpful recommending a famous local restaurant for dinner. He also offers to arrange a booking for us, explaining that usually bookings need to be made well in advance.

The hotel is quite small but it is beautiful. It is centred around a light internal courtyard with a very ornate cast iron spiral staircase running up to the bedrooms on the floors above. I wonder about the mix of styles but like most buildings of its age it has clearly been repurposed over the years.

There are touches of Chinese, Peranakan, that Chinese Malay blend we will explore later, as well as art deco features, and the black and white tiles give it a cool colonial feel. Mr Ibrahim tells us that before the war it had been six traditional shop houses but after the war it was converted to a single grand dwelling for one large, very wealthy family.

Today it is a restored heritage project which celebrates the diverse cultural history of the city and it is currently owned by a large soft drinks company. He tells us that we will find samples of their products including various cold tea beverages in our room later, all of which will be complimentary.

Our stay here will be short, too short as it turns out,

but once we have caught our breath we head out into the street. Despite the cultural sights we witnessed coming here, our priority is a bit more basic, for now it is simply to find something to eat. We head down to the junction with Jonker Street which is fortunately only about a hundred yards away.

Jonker Street is the focus of the old town, famed for its Friday night market which will be tomorrow night, and we can see that it is already covered from end to end with Chinese lanterns.

This is quite a spectacle even by day but I am looking forward to seeing it lit up in the evening. At the junction we find a rough concrete building with plastic tables and chairs and a steady stream of customers going in and out so it looks like a good bet.

The Chinese server fortunately speaks some English helping us order a couple of dishes. In my case at least, despite his best efforts at describing it, I have no idea what to expect. I am soon presented with a clay pot filled with a bubbling bright yellow sauce. I can clearly make out noodles, a boiled egg, cut red chillies and he hands me a little soup spoon with a serving of Sambal, the spicy chilli paste that seems to be an essential accompaniment to every meal here, but the rest is a mystery.

I must be pulling some faces because Sue is laughing at my obvious discomfort but I persevere. After all, I came here to try everything. Besides, I only have two choices...eat or don't. I am pleased to report that it was the right decision as lunch was delicious.

As a rule, I like to be able to identify what I am eating and to have a fair idea of what it was when it was either alive or growing, depending on the food group but this is definitely not the case here. As it turns out I am not partial to the suspiciously, and rather too generically named 'fish balls,' but tofu I don't mind.

It was so good that after lunch we buy some of the homemade Sambal paste before heading off in the wrong direction to find the river and getting ourselves quite lost. It's all part of the fun of exploring and no problem to retrace our steps, doubling back along a busy road running parallel with Jonker street while we drink in the strange sights.

Eventually we find our target and as we cross a small bridge to get a better view down the river, we get our first glimpse of a large monitor lizard relaxing in the sunshine. These 'dustbins of the river' are scavengers and will literally eat anything but they seem to thrive and can grow to over six feet in length.

They don't actively seek interaction with people but they are clearly clever enough to know how wasteful we are. Despite not being aggressive, they do seem just a little bit menacing to us. Whilst their teeth and very large claws look prehistoric, the main risk from them is a blow from their long tails which they can use like a whip, if they feel threatened.

Looking down the along river, its banks are lined with a colourful array of old shop houses that are in various states of repair. Some have been turned in to trendy wine bars and even the Hard Rock café has a presence here.

On the other side of the river is Red Square. Imaginatively named after the red hue of the buildings. Its centre pieces are the Protestant Christ Church, the old government building, and the fountain, built in 1904 in honour of Queen Victoria.

This is the centre of Melaka that most tourist brochures will highlight.

A little farther away is the white Catholic Cathedral of St Francis which is apparently a replica of the Montpelier cathedral in France. Ironically though, due to the monochrome decorations of the buildings, the historical 'European' centre is probably the least colourful part of the city that we have seen so far.

We don't linger too long. It is already late afternoon. Our plan is to get cleaned up then to take a night time cruise along the river to help us get our bearings, but it is hot so we head to the ice cream stall on the river bank and Sue has her first taste of Cendol (Chen Doll) on this trip.

Cendol is an interesting dessert. Although ingredients seem to vary this one is made with crushed ice, noodles that have the appearance of little green worms, coconut milk, palm sugar and a type of soft red mung bean. It's not quite liquid but not quite set.

No, I don't understand it either!

RIVER OR A CANAL?

We have been in Malaysia a week now and although the heat is still draining, the acclimatisation process is working well enough for us to both notice, and appreciate, the slightly cooler evening air.

Making our way to the jetty for the boat trip along the river, it becomes apparent that this must be the number one tourist attraction as it is heaving with both Chinese and Malay tourists.

As we boarded the fibreglass river boat, I was looking forward to a leisurely forty-minute cruise and to learning a little more about the old town, but I was about to be disappointed. We are crammed in like sardines and the boat set off like a jet ski.

"Blimey" I thought "there must be some ground to cover if we are going to be belting along like this."

The first bridge loomed into view overhead in what seemed like an instant.

It was brightly lit reflecting all of the colours of the rainbow from its iron railings onto the arc of water below. Then as if not to be outdone by the visual inputs to my eyes, my ears began to ache as a cacophony of sound erupted all around me.

The music began and the guide raced through numerous announcements in four different languages (very impressive by the way) trying to keep up with the speed of the sights coming and going as we flew by them.

Then somehow the volume seemed to go up and up. Her voice got louder and louder as if competing with the music and all of the passengers in turn seemed to shout as they tried to make themselves heard to one another.

I soon gave up any attempt at trying to understand what the guide was saying and simply formed my own impressions on the journey.

The river at this point is very uniform, maybe fifty feet wide with the banks all reinforced with concrete which gave it very much the appearance of a man-made canal rather than a natural river.

This had clearly once been a working port area; there were tell-tale signs not just from the buildings but in places the bank was tiered like a staircase where the ships of long ago would have loaded and unloaded their precious cargos.

It was like sailing along a rainbow river as the tree lined banks were also illuminated. It is very cleverly done and makes every tree look like it's very own rainbow bridge, reaching from the river up into the night sky.

We reach the midway point where I immediately suspect our river pilot must have been blinded by the incredible lightshow because he or she slams on the anchors and hits nearly every object possible as we turn before beginning our sprint back up the river. I hang on with one hand to avoid falling overboard, trying to take some photos as we pass by what looks like a monorail system, a Ferris wheel, and Kampong Morten.

A kampong is a small village or settlement, typically with houses on stilts. This one is regarded as a living museum as many people still practice the traditional lifestyle here and it is now a tourist attraction.

I now have a headache. I am beginning to understand why news programmes put warning notices on about programs that contain flash photography.

Twenty minutes later, shell shocked and partially deaf, we disembark and make our way back along Jonker street to grab a bite to eat before heading back to the hotel. Jonker street is surprisingly quiet but we do find small restaurant where we enjoy some crab cakes and various light bites.

Breakfast the next morning in the Liu Men is quite light but I take the opportunity to take on copious amounts of liquid, tea obviously. I also have a few bits of fruit from the continental buffet and can't resist ordering some dhal curry sauce with homemade roti.

It will help us if we figure out a plan for the day. Scrolling through our phones to see what sense we could make of the things we had seen the previous evening we decided to anchor our day with a reservation at the Peranakan restaurant that Mr Ibrahim had recommended but when I found it and tried to book a table I suddenly realised what he had been trying to tell us. This was going to be tricky but the hotel staff said not to worry, that they would organise it for us before we returned later in the day, and we headed out, once again following the river.

Although they are painted in many different colours, the shop houses look slightly less glamourous without their multicolour lightshow but they do offer an interesting insight into life here, both past and present.

As we continue our walk into the more modern part of the city there are young children fishing here who are keen to talk to us and show off their skills.

As we watch, one of the boys, maybe ten years old, pulls a triangular shaped fish from the water. It is perhaps six inches across and he adds it to the small bucket which already contains around half a dozen similar creatures.

I ask him if he fishes for sport but he says "no, they are good to eat" and they will be going home with him to be made into fish soup.

There are many more in the river below, glistening in the sunlight and lurking not far away I also spy a 'dustbin of the river' which watches patiently, perhaps hoping for some scraps.

I admire their enterprise here but the sight caught me off guard. I had expected to see this in the rural parts of the country where I know the jungle still provides a lot of food in some places, but the scene here, in the middle of a modern city with high rise buildings to either side of us seems strangely out of both place and time.

Making our way to the strange looking houses we had passed by last night we again come across Kampong Morten. Unsurprisingly these houses on stilts have a lot in common with the houses in Bali and the rest of Indonesia, as this where the Malay people came from.

Prior to the invention of roads or the paving and shoring up of the riverbanks, they would have provided some protection from the monsoon flooding whilst also giving some shelter for the animals below the living accommodation.

Almost all of them are still inhabited and most now have modern enhancements to make life easier, but there is one house which is kept in its original form. It is really only this one rather than the whole Kampong that serves as a living museum, but we would like to see inside it and scout around to see if there is a way in.

Unfortunately, it seems to be locked up at the moment. One of the neighbours sees us looking around and explains that the owner is at Friday prayers and is unlikely to open today. Almost as if to underline the point I can hear the Iman calling the faithful to prayer, his voice quietly wafting across the city.

It does sounds suspiciously like he is chanting "better luck next time!"

The best option now is to head back along the river to Red (Dutch) Square and grab something to eat.

On the way we pass a shop that proudly announces that is sells BUM equipment. The mind boggles but we can't help laughing and a fascination with the signage begins as we wait to see what other smutty double-entendres will present themselves over the next week or so.

It's not as if there isn't enough to see but we reason that it does no harm to keep one's mind active.

To the rear of red square there is a small air museum and just beyond that there is another museum. This is a replica of the sultan's palace and we try to get in, but it is just closing for the afternoon so the other option is to climb the hill overlooking the square and head to the old ruined church of St Paul instead.

It is a hard climb in the heat, even though its probably less than two hundred metres but it is well worth it. From up here the views stretch from Little India in one direction all the way down the river to the Malacca straights in the other.

For the Muslim population, Friday is a quiet day of prayers and refection, but not for everyone else. The famous Jonker street market will be our focus for this evening and by late afternoon the stalls are already being set up.

I need a shower but I can't resist looking in the Chinese Temple which is just across the road from our hotel first. I am not sure if they are worshippers, or some kind of temple officials but the people inside are surprisingly welcoming.

The courtyard inside is full of concrete statues of Dragons with a line of red and yellow lanterns that draw the eye to three cauldrons. These contain the smouldering incense sticks left as offerings to the ancestors. I can see on the other side of the cauldrons people swaying back and forth offering their silent prayers in the inner temple.

I don't want to intrude but it can't hurt to buy some incense sticks and offer our own silent prayers before heading back.

Just as they had promised, the concierge kindly confirms that dinner at the Peranakan Mansion restaurant is booked. It is early at 6.30pm but that gives us plenty of time to enjoy the night market later.

This restaurant is something of an institution in Melaka and our first real taste of Peranakan style. As its name suggests it is situated in what would once have been a very wealthy family house, a proper Mansion.

The style is very exotic to western eyes more used to a muted colour pallet, but no doubt sophisticated and glamourous to eastern eyes who are more at home with the vibrancy evident all around us.

The colours are vivid. Partially hidden, behind

ornately carved dark hard wood panelling and decorated with golden Chinese symbols, a plum cast iron spiral staircase rises to the upper floors where more brightly coloured screens offer some privacy. Over the atrium hang crystal chandeliers that look impossibly heavy for the thin steel fittings.

Most of the tables are large, round, complete with lazy Susan's, and they are clearly aimed at large family gatherings. Sure enough, not long after we are seated the place is awash with families whose tables are soon filled with the most fantastic looking dishes.

The food was delicious but with hindsight we would

have been better eating here on a different day.

When we finally do step out on to Jonker street it is heaving, aided by the fact that it is now fully pedestrianised for the evening along its six hundred or so metre length.

All kinds of foods are on offer here. The hawkers are interspersed amongst the usual stalls selling various trinkets and knick knacks, most of which is clearly aimed at tourists or children. It is a lovely sight non the less and a pleasant stroll in the warm evening air along a lantern lined street, thronging with people.

I normally prefer to stay away from crowds but after lockdown you can sense the optimism in the air, the joy of ordinary people around you. It is heightened by the Lunar New Year celebrations and the children are captivated by Chinese dancers on the makeshift stage. You cannot help but share the sense of optimism for the approaching New Year.

A FELLOW PILGRIM

It's Saturday morning. Today is Chinese New Year's Eve and we need to be in Kuala Lumpur before nightfall if there is any hope of us spending the evening in Chinatown, which we expect will be buzzing tonight. We are really looking forward to witnessing some intense celebrations.

After checking out, I use the Grab app to order a car, this time not bothering with the cab companies because I know we are going over the state line again. It is quite early but fortunately I manage to secure a decent price for the ninety-mile trip.

All too soon our trip to Melaka is over as a battered old, red, Perodua Bezza car pulls up outside the hotel and a small Chinese lady, maybe in her mid-twenties gets out to greet us.

If you want to get a real sense of the people and way of life in a foreign country, then travel by the same means the locals use whether that is the bus, a taxi, or the train. It is well worth using the taxis here in Malaysia as the drivers invariably prove to be amongst the most interesting and informative people that you can chat with. Our driver today, Melissa, is no exception.

She is bright and cheerful from the moment she says hello. Even though only her brown eyes are visible behind the obligatory mask; you can tell that she is smiling.

We are no sooner on the road when she starts expertly quizzing us about our journey. So good are her interrogation techniques that by the time we stop for petrol five minutes later, she literally knows Sue's life story.

When she returns, we make our way through the suburbs to the motorway and she points out various places of interest, such as the government buildings and the zoo, which she enthusiastically gives a thumbs up to, should we ever decide to visit again.

As we hit the motorway, a pleasant surprise awaits. Melissa tells us that they are all toll free for the holiday weekend so although I had been concerned about travelling on New Year's Eve, it looks like we picked a good day to travel after all.

I suppose we all have an unconscious bias, and even though I know that this is a progressive and tolerant Muslim country, I confess that I was surprised when Melissia had turned up. When I mention it to her that female taxi drivers, even in the UK, are few and far between she just shrugs. She raises her hand, rubbing her fingers together, indicating money.

We all need to live she says and then immediately gives us a run-down of that Chinese pragmatism and work ethic that binds their culture and families together. Her own life story is a fascinating prism which will allow us to view our explorations into the past in a much more personal light.

Melissa has a daughter, just over a year old and although she currently lives in Melaka, her husband, who is a little older than her and drives a taxi too, lives in Kuala Lumpur. This journey for her is one she knows well, as she has spent the last two years during lockdown living in Kuala Lumpur whilst her daughter, almost from the day she was born, has been cared for by her grandmother in Melaka.

This sounds strangely familiar and I wonder about how long it takes a culture to change. On the surface, even in this part of the world, people are much better off materially but how much has really changed here since the 1920's?

In the West, furlough had cushioned the blow for many working people but that was not the case here and real sacrifices had to be made.

I can sense that there is a tinge of regret in her voice, but she laughs as she explains that her daughter is so attached to her grandmother that when they go on holiday she always has to come along. To not know one's parents as people is one thing, but for your parents to be literal strangers, as had been the case for Lily, is almost too hard to contemplate.

Although we are strangers, I find myself hoping that Melissa is making up for lost time now that the lockdown is over. As if she is reading my mind as she talks, she pulls out a mobile phone from nowhere and starts scrolling through photos and media clips to show us.

The phone was a complete surprise as she already had a phone on the windscreen with a speed camera app on it. Her daughter is beautiful, but the phone is handed back quickly so that she can concentrate on the road but she says not to worry.

I have nagging doubts about the impact of technology and social media on young people, but this is one example where it has the potential to be a really powerful emotional bridge between family members.

Melissa, it seems has embraced the convenience of technology whole heartedly. I am sure she is smiling when she says that she often watches movies whilst driving if she is alone and it's quiet. Perhaps she is kidding us, but we look at one another sitting in the back and decide it best to keep the conversation going. Neither of us want her to get bored on this trip so we continue to ask her about her life.

She works hard, and she has a plan to buy a new car soon. A larger one, perhaps an MPV that will allow her to earn more for her family and presumably one with more USB charging points.

She is young. Maybe we shouldn't be so personal but I ask if she has plans for more children to which she replies with an emphatic "no." She confesses that the pain of childbirth is not something she wants to go through again but in any event the idea of large families in this community is now an old fashioned one.

It is easy to understand why people want more financial security but sadly, the people here are at risk of being infected with the same sickness that pervades the West. Both parents have to work to provide the standard of living that modern life 'demands.'

Melissa is a delight. She is full of surprises and tells us that she was in fact raised as a Roman Catholic.

I have come across Roman Catholics from the Indian Sub-Continent in the past, mainly from Goa where the Portuguese had long held territory but I have never encountered a Chinese Roman Catholic.

I find the subject of religion fascinating and I had noticed some vaguely religious things in the car but none of them struck me as Catholic.

"They're not" she explained. "I think I was quite rebellious as a child and my parents were at their wits end with me. I think my religion was something that did not suit my temperament so I have converted to Buddhism. It has really helped me calm down a lot."

I am not entirely sure what that means but her current circumstances are testament to the fact that she has clearly grown up a lot since those days. She has a twinkle in her eye though when she tells us she still likes to go away for trips with her girlfriends.

Langkawi is the destination of choice as it is easy to get to, a short flight of an hour or so from Kuala Lumpur and most importantly the alcohol is duty free. Johnny Walker Black label is the drink of choice and every traveller can bring back one litre, even the smallest children.

I cannot help but smile at the thought that here we are, all together in the same car, with so many differences between us, yet underneath we all crave the same things. It seems that Melissa is a pilgrim too and in that regard her occupation suits her. It is almost a symbol of her own very personal journey to find herself and for meaning in life. Her biggest ambition is to visit Tibet.

"The Potala Palace?" I ask.

"Yes, the home of the Dalai Llama, at least before his exile."

Is she sharing her journey with us or are we sharing our journey with her? I don't know but I am so glad to have met her; she has given me a great deal to think about.

I have a theory that the only difference between the religions of the east and the west is the way they are expressed and that there must be a common source. If there is only one source, logically there can only be one true religion so the different ways of expressing it may well be just to accommodate our different cultural temperaments. I must confess though, that I had never before come across so vivid an example.

Although I don't yet know it, despite our very brief encounter we will carry Melissa with us on our journey and in a few days, I will get a chance to reflect on this conversation again.

As we talked and drove north, the clouds gathered overhead. They gradually darkened and soon the rain began. Although it rains everyday here, outside of the rainy season you can count on it to be just a short downpour then to dry up quickly.

The forecast this morning for our destination however was for prolonged and heavy rain. Sure enough the closer we got to KL the heavier the rain became. The carriageways began to take on a glassy appearance and we can see the motorbike riders seeking shelter under any bridges they came across.

Rather alarmingly the trend we had witnessed on the way up from Johor Bharu, of traffic flowing in the opposite direction seems to be, if anything, intensifying. On the final approach into Kuala Lumpur, it is now clear that any person of Chinese origin, or with any Chinese connection whatsoever is literally fleeing in any direction possible, as long as it is away from the city.

We are concerned for Melissa's return journey but she is not fazed. She will at least see her husband and while the queues and torrential rain remain, she assures us that will not head back. As we say goodbye to Melissa, I can't help hoping that her parents are proud of her, indeed I am sure they are. She reminds me of our own daughters, unorthodox at times perhaps, but hard working, resourceful and resilient certainly.

It is comforting to know that they have everything they need within themselves to overcome whatever life throws at them.

KUALA LUMPUR

The Sheraton Imperial Hotel is a typical five-star business hotel. It is in places tired and in need of a little TLC but otherwise it is well appointed in terms of the facilities it has.

It offers access to a gym, bars, restaurants, and an outdoor swimming pool, which rather bizarrely is closed when it rains. The rooms are comfortable, the bathrooms enormous and the high floors offer great views over the city to the hills beyond, which is the only thing about the hotel that lets you know you are here, rather than any other city.

The impression I have of Kuala Lumpur itself is that it is a poor man's version of Singapore. The Skyline of skyscrapers are just as impressive but it is a veritable concrete jungle in a much more visceral sense. It's an environment where people live, and yet it seems to have been built with absolutely no thought for its inhabitants.

Pavements are not a given. There are some, but they are not consistent neither are they well maintained. The roads are wide but there are no obvious underpasses or bridges. You literally have to take your life in your hands if you want to cross six, or sometimes eight lanes of traffic. If you do manage to cross at a junction where there are traffic lights, they stay on a matter of a few seconds, only long enough for a quick sprint before the traffic is rolling once again.

The metro is not as simple as it is in Singapore either. The stations are in the middle of the road but you can't use them as a safe thoroughfare to walk over to the other side without paying.

Instead of buying a ticket you buy a token which you have to deposit at your destination to exit the station; but if you are changing lines, it seems quite complicated and we can't figure out how to achieve this with one token so you quickly lose the will to live. Maybe that is why you have to run across the road…if offers a way out of life for those who can't figure out the metro.

Basically, this means that whenever you leave the hotel you need to get a taxi, so after a quick scrub up we order one and head for the Petaling Street Market in Chinatown. When we arrive, it is getting dark and the tourists are starting to arrive. The Chinese lanterns lining the streets add colour to the proceedings but there are only a relatively few market stalls open. We visited here many years ago and the usual mass of hawkers and food stalls are nowhere to be seen.

As we wander through the main street, I can see down a dimly lit side street all the stacked tables, chairs and stall frames from the eateries and the shadows seem to be dancing beneath them. I look for a little longer and as my eyes adapt to the dim lighting, I realise they are not shadows at all, dozens of rats are playing happily amongst all the furniture. The rats are huge and frankly I would only give a cat a fifty-fifty chance in an encounter.

I know it is off putting but it's just one of those

facts of life. Where people live, because humans are such a wasteful species, rats inevitably will flourish. Unfortunately, with those thoughts still playing in my mind it is becoming a necessity to find somewhere to eat.

Just outside of the market we find a busy looking place and plead for a table. We are fortunate to be seated just before a long queue appears outside and the heavens open once again leaving people scrambling to take shelter under the awning.

In short, the New Year celebrations that we had anticipated were nowhere to be seen, so after dinner we decided to head into a dessert only restaurant nearby before heading back to our hotel.

This was a real consolation treat because I encountered for the first time Ginger Milk. In a rather elaborate ceremony, a bowl of pressed ginger is brought to the table with a teapot, a saucer, and an old-fashioned egg timer which is filled with pink sand.

Hot milk is poured from the teapot over the ginger, the saucer is placed over the bowl and the egg timer is upended. Our server advises us to leave it until the timer is finished so that the 'enzyme' in the mixture can do its work.

I have no idea what the 'enzyme' is, but a few minutes later the result is a revelation. So much so that it makes an otherwise disappointing trip to Chinatown all seem worthwhile.

I know I could call a Grab car when we leave but we had noticed a taxi rank around the corner so we decided to take a few steps to walk off dessert. When I ask at the rank for a price of the return trip to the hotel, I am a little annoyed that it is going to be thirty Ringgits. It was half that to get here so I haggled and eventually agreed on twenty ringgits.

It was a good-natured exchange though. The taxi rank manager laughed as he called over a taxi driver and said. "If you want to speak to him you will have to talk to his left ear".

"Why?" I asked.

"Because he is deaf in the other one." he said.

Of course he is. "Oh, alright" I replied.

The driver seemed completely oblivious to our conversation making me wonder if it would matter which ear I spoke into, but he was a nice, older guy.

As we turned in for the night, I couldn't help smiling to myself. We had only been arguing over two quid. I enjoyed the haggling just on principle but I tipped the driver anyway when we arrived so it made no difference in the end.

Breakfast in the hotel restaurant on New Years' Day was utter chaos. The place was bouncing, kids were running around everywhere and although the Chinese had left town, the Malays were clearly making the most of the long holiday weekend.

What is normally quite a civilised experience was today a bit like feeding the farm animals from a series of troughs. In the end we just sat down with some fruit, tea and coffee and tried to figure out what to do next.

Kuala Lumpur does have its share of shopping malls and some of these are very high end. The two most famous are probably the Suria which sits below the Petronas Twin Towers, and The Pavilion.

It is ironic that my trip here is partly to take a break from the modern world we live in. I don't think many of us pause long enough to realise how powerful and full on our lives are. Yes, this brings pressure but it can also be extremely helpful and I soon get a lesson from a friend, Elaine, who lives in Australia as to just how helpful it can be.

Elaine lives in Perth; Western Australia and she has been following our journey through Sue's Instagram posts and messages. Normally there is a very large time difference, but coincidentally we're now in the same time zone making real time communication a practical proposition.

Sue had mentioned our disappointment with the muted celebrations we had seen so far. We had expected to see fireworks and lion or dragon dancers on every street corner. We should be fighting the buggers off for goodness' sake, but we had not seen any.

Elaine is well versed in Chinese culture having spent many years living in Hong Kong and previously being married to a Chinese national. She recommended that we head to The Pavillion shopping centre, telling us we would definitely see one there. Thank you, Elaine!

I had briefly toyed with the idea of trying to walk somewhere but it quickly wore off. It is still raining outside and it doesn't look like it is going to get any better so I order a taxi. Once again fate was about to play a blinder for us as she guided us on this journey.

The traffic is heavy in the city in spite of the Chinese exodus and soon we are at a complete standstill. Our driver Mr Gan is a lovely, older Chinese gentleman. He is keen to chat. His English is good but I suspect he may have learned it later in life because he still has that faintly comical pronunciation.

We move a few hundred yards then come to a standstill yet again. Mr Gan is shuffling uncomfortably in his seat and a moment later he farts. "Oh, velly solly" he says and winds the window down waving his hands with an almost comical gesture that would suggest we were being gassed.

We are wearing the obligatory masks and find it quite funny. It is also slightly ironic that, now the windows are open, we stand more chance of being gassed by the traffic outside of the vehicle.

He's a real professional though and quickly moves the conversation on asking us about our plans for our next destination, wondering if we need a taxi.

"Yes, we do actually."

We like him and would be quite happy to use him again but when we are due to leave in a couple of days he is already booked for a trip to the Genting Highlands.

I am not concerned as I am getting quite used to the

Grab app, (although I am little tired of all the texts offering me half price burgers and free pizza delivery with my first order), but Mr Gan tells me to leave it with him and as he drops us off, I think no more of it and head off in to the 'Pavillion.'

This looks promising. As well as the obligatory 'happy new year' sign there is large display set up that looks like it may be a stage and we quickly confirm that there will indeed be Lion Dance performed here in a few hours' time. In the meantime Sue wants to explore the shopping centre.

To a lot of women this may somehow offer the prospect of magical new vistas, filled with previously unimagined wonders, but to most men it looks like any other shopping centre. Indeed it looks identical to every other one that we have been in since we first landed in Singapore.

Not to be put off, we set off to explore and Sue peruses the shops while I console myself with the continuing stream of double-entendres that the shop names provide.

'Ichi Zen' for example…. there must be a cream for that!

Sue meanwhile is having her own little voyage of discovery into the world of cheap Chinese 'tat'. She seems to be very excited by a few of the things on sale so I go inside and see what all the fuss is about. Normally I don't mind too much what she buys, she is generally right and has good taste but her Chinese ancestry seems to be taking over, leaving me with no choice but to intervene.

I am forced to draw the line at a small pot cat with one waving arm (paw) which is designed to go on the dashboard of the car. I have visions of getting home and people flagging us down thinking we are taxi or stopping at a set of lights then someone jumping in the back seat and telling me to go the football stadium, or worse starting a conversation by asking me what time I get off.

She is obviously gutted by my apparent lack of taste, "but it's colourful" she protests "and look they come in all sizes." Indeed they do, I glance around the shelves full of happy looking pot cats staring back at me hopefully, but sanity prevails and we head back out to the main atrium of the shopping centre.

When you are in surroundings like this, there is very little that would tell you whether you were in the East or the West or indeed one country or another. One thing that marks Malaysia out is the Royal Selangor pewter that is made on the outskirts of Kuala Lumpur. We take the opportunity to visit the large store they have here to view their wares and to enquire about the possibility of a factory visit and tour.

The workmanship is truly exquisite and I explain to the lady behind the counter that, tomorrow perhaps it would be a joy to watch something so beautiful being handmade.

She smiles awkwardly. I think she is trying to let us down gently but there was no easy way to put and, in the end, she blurted out … "you can't it's closed."

"Closed" I repeated making sure I had heard correctly.

"Yes "she said, "the workers there are mainly Chinese and they won't be back at work for a few more days." Then she added hopefully that the shop we were currently in had everything the little gift shop at the factory had. Let's be honest, it's not the same though is it? Who doesn't love a little gift shop?

Exhausted from walking what seemed like miles and deflated by the latest setback, it was time to get something to eat and once again to revise our itinerary. In fairness one thing the shopping centres here are really good at providing is a quality food hall and the 'Pavillion' is no exception. We sit down in the Royal India Restaurant where we enjoy a fabulous meal of Southern Indian and Goan dishes.

Perhaps the food was evoking something deep inside me or perhaps it was just a coincidence but there is a large Hindu temple of the outskirts of the city so I suggested making that our destination for tomorrow instead.

At the appointed time we find a good place amongst the growing crowd from to watch the Lion dance. When the anticipated start time comes and goes the large crowd is clearly beginning to get a bit restless.

I have no where I need to be, so I am happy to wait. Then I get a WhatsApp message from Mr Gan. He has a friend who is free when we need to go to the airport to collect our hire car and asks if it is ok to give him my number? – Yes please.

Eventually the Lion dancers sneak in via a rear entrance making their way surreptitiously into what I can only describe as a small, rather ornate, little shed that has been made to look like a little house in a forest. I can see their bright orange, yellow and red costumes from the balcony, but the restless crowd down in front of the stage are still none the wiser.

Then without warning the drumming begins and the air is suddenly filled with a sense of anticipation as the crowd falls silent.

The dancing is fantastic. The stage seemed to be very small with lots of little flat topped, mock trees in the way. Two lions, each with two dancers made their way through the forest garden and danced directly in front of the crowd to the delight of the many small children. Then they turned as if to retrace their steps but one by one they climbed onto the flat-topped poles, jumping from one to another, continuing their intricate dance.

The tops were round, several feet apart but no more than the size of a dinner plate. I had not anticipated the level of skill or sheer athleticism. Simply walking across these would be hard enough without the encumbrance of a large costume and having to be bent double like a pantomime horse, but they were jumping and dancing, twisting back and forth, staging mock lion fights at the same time.

The whole scene was quite mesmerising. The sound of the rhythmic drumming, the brightness of the costumes mixed with the gasps of the children was a heady mixture.

It is easy to understand why this draws the mind to Chinese mythology. For the children watching this is probably the equivalent of what old fairy tales would be to western kids. Magical indeed.

By the time it is finished it is getting quite late and it will be another early start tomorrow so we decide to head back to the hotel for a light snack in the bar before retiring for the night.

THE BATU CAVES

To be honest despite the weather and the difficulty in walking anywhere, the longer we are in Kuala Lumpur, the more we are settling into the place and, I am almost loathe to admit it but, the more it is growing on me.

Our final day would turn out to be the most interesting by far. After breakfast we take the short taxi ride to the Batu caves where, by nine o clock, it is already heaving. The temple complex itself is free to enter, but not for cars so our driver drops us off nearby then he points us in the general direction of the entrance before bidding us a good day.

The first thing you notice as you enter the temple complex is the massive golden statue of Lord Murugan that seems to be guarding the multi coloured steps to the left, which rise like a huge, four lane highway to the cave entrance high above. The cave entrance is shaped like the tip of the spear that the statue is holding and adds an interesting symmetry to the whole scene.

It's not just the size of the thing that hits you. It's also the colours, the sounds of the devotees chanting and the aromas in the air from the stalls and cafés between the entrance and the foot of the grand stairway that seem to overwhelm every sense.

For the first time since we arrived in Kuala Lumpur the sun came out and we could see that there are many stalls, caves, and temples here. It would take some time to explore it all and before we even reach the bottom of the stairs, we are accosted by numerous hawkers selling bits of tat, jewellery made of string, cheap plastic, and wire. I am soon one hundred ringgits poorer and we are both wearing copper-coloured bracelets and red and black necklaces in honour of our ethereal host Lord Murugan.

The vendor assures me that they will bring us nothing but good luck, strength, and power. I did haggle of course and to us, a hundred ringgit is only a few quid, but the salesman left very happy so I am fairly sure that I have been robbed.

There is something about every religion the world over that one way or another manages to relieve visitors of their hard-earned cash but like all the other pilgrims I take it in good grace, cross my fingers, and hope he is right.

At the bottom of the staircase, you really get a sense of just how big the structure is. The golden statue is the largest in Malaysia at one hundred and forty feet high and seems strangely out of scale next to the two hundred and seventy-two painted concrete steps that seem to disappear into the distance above. It looks like a rainbow bridge. ..... an oriental version of 'Bifrost' from Norse Mythology.

We had been careful to dress respectfully but at the bottom of the stairs many people were taking off their shoes. We had been walking miles every day since we arrived in Singapore. I had open blisters on my feet from my new shoes and the stairs were filthy so I asked one of the locals if I would be able to continue.Fortunately, he said "yes."

I would be able to go into the cave but I would not be able to enter the shrine itself, so we set off, drinking in the sights as we climbed. Some of our fellow travellers were in bare feet, others in yellow or orange robes and ash covered faces climbed on their knees, and still more carried pots on their heads full of offerings

The experience is made all the more surreal as our climb is overseen not just by the statue at our side but by nature herself. Birds and bats are flying overhead and monkeys are everywhere, some scrambling though the vegetation that grows from the cliff wall and yet more walking up the handrails beside us that seem to act as chaperones for the newly initiated.

At the top of the staircase, you enter a huge limestone cavern where inside, there is another temple building and numerous smaller shrines built into rock alcoves. The cave is bathed in natural light. Sunlight streams in from the 'windows' above where the roof has in places collapsed in the long distant past due to untold centuries of water ingress.

Sue leaves her shoes outside the temple and heads inside but as I wander around outside, I realise that it is the cave itself, not the building, which is the real temple.

The cave had been used for mining bat and bird

guano for fertiliser but the Tamils who migrated here from southern India began to use the cave in the late nineteenth century for worship. It is said that they were inspired by the spear tip shaped opening which they recognized as a sign of Lord Murugan, the Hindu God of War.

They have been transforming this and the other caves ever since. The notion of a temple to a God of War seems strangely incongruous to me as, even amongst the throng of people and animals, this is such a serene and peaceful place.

I can't help thinking of Melissa here, of her spiritual quest and noticing the many similarities between the east and the west.

I wonder if India is the real source of it all. Most of western religions including Judaism, Christianity and Islam have at least some of their roots in Mosaic lore (Moses). The Kaballah talks of four realms, Atziluth, Briah, Yetzirah and Assiah.

Sometimes they are described as alternatively 'Spirit, Emotion, Mental and Physical' or even as the four elements, Fire, Water, Air and Earth.

What most people do not realise is that this is where we get the four suits of our everyday playing cards. Clubs represents fire or spirit, Hearts represent water or emotions, Spades represent Air or thought and Diamonds represent Earth or the physical plane.

This, combined with different interpretations of the numbers is how they are used for divination by 'fortune tellers' if you believe in that sort of thing.

Here I am, in the orient eight thousand miles from home looking at an alcove with four statues. One holding a wand, (fire) one with a flower cup (water), one riding a peacock (air) and one that is part elephant (earth).

In another alcove I recognize yet another statue, this one carrying a bag over his shoulder on a stick, with a cockerel accompanying him. This is the 'fool' of the western Tarot tradition about to incarnate on earth, bringing his animal, nature, and his bag of unredeemed Karma with him.

I love this place. It is like a book, there is so much to see and learn if only we had more time but we have already been here for several hours and soon Sue is back, calling me and it is time to head back down the steps to get something to eat.

I had seen a small restaurant near the entrance on the way in but before we head inside Sue wants to visit the temple at the bottom of the steps.

I stand outside to wait patiently and pretty soon I am surrounded by a veritable sea of shoes and sandals. It is getting very busy here now and I am being slowly marinated in the smell of exotic spices wafting its way in my direction from the nearby kitchen.

The 'restaurant' is rather basic, it looks more like a school canteen hidden in the back of a supermarket store room. There are boxes, bottles, and pallets everywhere.

All the food here is vegetarian which we do not mind, and we soon have a plastic tray covered with rice and various types of bhajis and dhal and we are sharing a table with what we assume are a group of locals.

Although the food is spicy, washed down with cold water it is a welcome relief from the heat outside but it is not a particularly relaxing break. We cannot linger for long as there is a constant stream of diners anxious to relieve us of our plastic tray and seats, and besides there is a lot more to see.

Although the main cave is the grandest, there are in fact numerous caves here but unlike the main one, they are not all free. There simply is not enough time to visit them all but I would like to see at least one more. Before deciding which one, we head along the makeshift 'street' to explore the stalls selling peanuts, spices, snacks, Indian sweets, and the inevitable gifts.

I am not surprised when come across the same guy who had already relieved me of funds earlier in the day. He is actually very pleasant and he is keen for us to come and see his stall.

It is hard to know where to look next though and a little further on I am distracted again, this time by a statue of a rather large golden Eagle.

Sue is also distracted by the sound of music coming from another temple. She takes her shoes off, heads up the steps and she is enthusiastically welcomed by those in inside. I, meanwhile, am outside shaking my head reading the notice which provides details of the wedding celebration that Sue has just crashed!

It's not every day you get to see a Hindu wedding. Despite the lack of an invitation I am pleased to report that she had a nice time and was particularly impressed with the multi coloured sand mandalas that had been created in honour of the event.

By the time she emerged I had spotted the very large statue of the green monkey god Hanuman near the entrance to the cave or Ramayana and decided this would be our last exploration here for today. Once again nature conspired with the statues to make this an unforgettable experience as dozens of monkeys sat patiently waiting for the tourists (that would be us) to peel bananas and satsumas to feed them.

They have nothing to fear here amongst a vegetarian community, food is donated daily and they took the offerings gently from our hands. We would feed them again later but now it was time to continue our exploration.

As the vendor of our necklaces had predicted, good luck was coming our way and he was right. We managed to get a discount on the entrance into the cave of Ramayana.

This cave tells the story of the Indian god Rama, and his quest to rescue his wife from the clutches of his rival Ravana, whilst he is incarnated in human form.

This cave has a different feel to the others. Apart from the giant statues of the gods outside, the Green Hanuman and the Blue Rama, it has the feel of a model village.

 Unlike the main cave this one is artificially lit, it is very colourful and as you follow the route inside the cave it tells the story in a series of vignettes, like three dimensional still scenes cut from a movie.

Once again, I am reminded of Melissa and the Catholic version of the Old Testament of the Bible with which she would have been familiar when I come across the statue of the sleeping giant. I am again struck by the similarity of the imagery and wonder at the source.

Genesis Chapter 6 says, ……" There were giants in the earth in those days, and also after that, when the sons of God came in unto the daughters of men, and they bare them children."

How strange these 'sons of God' may have been. Here they are depicted as part elephant, part monkey, some are green and others blue.

We are used to seeing fantastic stories brought to life in the cinema today but the stories I have seen today have been told and handed down for millennia. It is no wonder that our ancestors were enthralled by them.

By the time we left, we're both completely captivated by the Hindu culture here and the cheap tat we bought on the way in have become treasured possessions. I don't think that either of us had envisaged this. We came here to explore Sue's Chinese heritage and expected that this would simply be a pleasant diversion but how we underestimated the experience of it all.

DOWN TO EARTH WITH A BUMP

Back in the real world we decide to head back into central Kuala Lumpur on the metro. I would like to give it another go because it should be easier this time as we won't have the complication of changing lines to contend with. We had attempted to use the metro the day we arrived here but it was a disaster.

I am almost immediately regretting the decision to try again; this wasn't looking like a much better start as we discover that the ticket machines are not working. There are cashiers behind the counter which gives me hope but this is quickly dashed when they tell us that they cannot take cash.

The trains are not particularly frequent here either, about every forty minutes or so but at least this will gave us time to figure it out and to use the facilities before heading down to the platform. I know it is easier for men, but public toilets are becoming something of a specialist subject out here and judging by the unhappy look on Sue's face I am guessing that she has just had yet another a run in with a 'squat' toilet.

I meanwhile, have been having a bit more luck and corresponding with Mr Gan's friend about the arrangements for our transport to the car rental depot at the airport tomorrow morning. At least

I hope it's Mr Gan's friend and not some random WhatsApp conversation I have started.

Perhaps it is because of the intensity of the Hindu religion in this area and the desire to assert the state religion of Islam but this is one of the few places where I have noticed anything particularly restrictive. The platform is divided and has a clearly designated female only waiting area. It seems quite relaxed but we are respectful of the culture and move along the platform to stand together.

This station must either be the very end of this line, or be very near the end of the line, because once we are all on board the train heads back the way it came.

We then made the mistake of getting off at Sentral (Central) rather than Kuala Lumpur. For some reason it seemed logical to assume that Sentral station would be nearer the centre and the shops. It isn't, and given the previously identified issues around walking we decided to escape from the heat for a while, jumped into a taxi and headed back to the hotel for a rest and a much-needed shower.

The blessing of Murugan is working overtime because this also turns out to be a stroke of good luck as the driver, informative as ever, showed us Merdeka, or Independence Square, then 'old' Little India, (not to be confused with 'new' Little India), and finally the old colonial administrative centre of the city. In short, lots of useful information and tips which we would file away for use later that evening.

It had been a lovely sunny day but by six o'clock the dark clouds were threatening once again, and we headed out in search of an evening meal. This time the taxi drops us at Merdeka Square so that we could explore the old colonial buildings.

The Sultan Abdul Samad Building dominates the area. The architecture is Moorish in style and it overlooks the square at the front and the confluence of two rivers, the Klang, and the Gombak to the rear.

The walkway that runs along the bank is called 'The River of Life' and it is now a popular heritage trail where the architecture changes from the Moorish to old colonial, then to glass and concrete skyscrapers, and then back again.

In a very literal sense, the rivers are of course the source of life for any city and once this area would have been used as the main source of water, a place to wash both body and clothes and inevitably to flush away the waste that the community generated.

Even today it does not look particularly clean. The dustbins of the river, the large monitor lizards are still plentiful here but not that long ago, as late as the 1930s, crocodiles of around fifteen feet in length were regularly seen here too.

Whilst the city has been spending a lot of money over the last decade or so to bring this area back to life I would still not fancy washing or bathing here, even without the crocodiles.

The hunters at least would have been happy here, they could earn a good bounty if they shot one and whilst I know that does not sit well with modern sensibilities, just step back, and imagine your kids playing in a park with no fence and hungry animals looking for a child sized meal.

It feels oppressive here and it is not the heat. It seems that the place has a something of a sad atmosphere about it that I can't quite put my finger on. Then a little farther along I read a sign that says it was not uncommon for people who felt that they had seen enough of life, to end their sorrows here. It is not made clear whether the fall killed them, they drowned, or the crocodiles ate them, but combined with the dark skies above the atmosphere is rather bleak.

I can't help thinking what a strange day it has been. This other worldly shroud now hanging over us contrasts sharply with the spiritual joy of this morning's visit to Batu and I am only too happy to leave this place behind. On a more positive note, the walkways are a little better in this area, no doubt to suit the British civil servants back in the day, and the back streets are quiet now.

China Town is not too far away but we can feel the drops of rain in the air. Behind us there is now a column of raindrops clearly visible, failing from the black sky. The watermark they leave is visible on the ground. It is slowly heading our way across the square like a rising tide, so we only make it as far as 'old' Little India which is just a few hundred yards from Merdeka Square, before deciding to take shelter in a restaurant.

We never did find 'New Little India?'

Outside the heavens really opened up and rain is soon bouncing off the roads, cars and the odd umbrella which passes by the window, but inside we are once again exploring the cuisine of southern India.

The menu is incomprehensible so we study the pictures and eventually two mixed plates of vegetarian food arrived. Although they look appealing, I can't stomach the desserts, which are so sickly sweet they make me want to gag.

The Madras coffee does not help. I thought it was just a plain black coffee when it came, bubbling like lava in a small steel pot on a plate, but it must have been full of something like cane sugar as it tasted more like a syrup.

It is our last night here and Sue wants to see the Petronas Towers lit up one last time so we walked to Petaling Street in Chinatown first where I can't resist going back to the dessert shop for some more ginger milk to settle my stomach. Unfortunately, the market place itself is no busier than it had been on New Year's Eve two nights earlier, so we headed to the taxi rank to argue about the price for the ride to the twin towers.

Our taxi driver tonight has friends in London and surprisingly he tells us that he played professional football for a while. He certainly does have a good knowledge of the English leagues and before he lets us go; he offers his prediction for the Premier league relegation battle for this season. Southampton, Leicester and either Everton or West Ham.

If you should find yourself visiting Kuala Lumpur you are bound to visit the Petronas Towers, the Suria shopping centre below and the park to the rear but here's a tip. Don't waste your money on buying a ticket for the observation deck. It is not as high as you would imagine. You get better views over the city and the miniature jungle from the nearby 1380ft, saucer shaped Menara KL tower, which also boasts the added attraction of a revolving restaurant.

At night however the sight of the twin towers is indeed spectacular. Many, but not all of the shops are open in the evenings, and unless you particularly want to shop there, this is the best time to visit.

To the front of the building there are hundreds of people. Lots of professional photographers are taking pictures amongst the fountains for tourists with the towers in the background. It's a clever set up, they sell the link to the digital images and even take payment by credit card. The fountains cool the air here a little and they draw the eye like small rivers of mirrored glass towards the building that looms over them.

The towers themselves look like two great crystal sculptures or two giant chandeliers that reach upwards into the night sky, instead of downwards from a far-off ceiling.

At the rear of the building the park is full of families with small children and there are yet more fountains. The water is lit from below with rainbow-coloured lights and a centre piece of a huge Rabbit made of Golden coloured coins to celebrate the New Year watches over the proceedings.

Unfortunately, what with the heat, the humidity due to the recent rain, the proximity of the lake and lots of exposed flesh to feed upon on, this particular evening it also has a rather noticeable population of mosquitoes.

Even had it not been cloudy, I doubt that I would be able to see the stars here at night due to the light pollution but even that takes on an almost ethereal visage here. The colours are vibrant and constantly changing at ground level but higher up the white lights of the towers are reflected in the nearby glass skyscrapers.

It is not a clear picture; perhaps it is due to the shape of the glass, the building itself or maybe just the angle of the buildings to one another. Standing here in the park below it appears to be more like a reflection in a pool of water that is constantly being reshaped by the movement of a gentle breeze blowing across its surface.

A fitting end to a rather strange day, one that despite the mundane aspects of being in a large city, seems to have had me with one foot in this world and one foot in another.

NEV'S NEW BLOWPIPE

The following morning at 9.30am Mr Gan's friend arrives to take us to KL International Airport. He is a gentleman of a similar age, also pleasant, not as talkative. He never does tell us his name, but he is equally well informed regarding his trade.

He asks us what time our flight is and which terminal we need to be at. I explain that we are looking for Hawk Car Rental centre which, from the email, seems to be at Terminal One. "No, it isn't" he says, "It's at KLIA 2 but don't worry we will find it".

Then we head off into morning traffic as the clouds start to darken once again.

At this point it is probably worth taking a little detour into the Malaysian Motor industry. The two big domestic brands here are Perodua and Proton. Most of their cars are quite small, built to a budget to suit the domestic market and, by our very spoilt European standards they are rather underpowered and basic.

I was expecting a Perodua Bezza which Melissa had assured me was both very fuel efficient and better than the equivalent Proton Saga but an hour later here I was face to face with, what was presumably the most recent iteration of a little red Proton Saga.

It had about twenty thousand miles on the clock, a bent filler cap cover and more scratches than a Labrador with fleas but I took a video as evidence then set off around the car park and the terminal building to get a feel for it before trusting myself on a motorway.

On the plus side they drive on the left here, the same side of the road as we do and it was an automatic so I didn't have to worry about changing gear but where do I start on the downsides?

It had some horsepower, maybe in double figures who knows, but some of the horses seemed to be having a day off. Nought to sixty comes eventually and that seems to be the top speed too, at least it's the top speed that I feel safe driving at. In short, the perfect car for me as I will be driving like Miss Daisy while I am here, and she doesn't drive. But it doesn't end there.

It rattles, it does not have built in sat nav so the 'Tom Tom' wires plugged into the cigarette lighter are in the way whenever I reach for anything. I can feel every wrinkle in the road through my backside, and they don't just do 'wrinkles' out here.

It's hard to find the lights, there are no automatic settings for anything, and apart from the fun of working yourself to death driving it with no modern safety aids, entertainment comes in the form of a radio and a CD player.

"Does anyone still have CDs?" I ask.

Sue shakes her head.

Well, I don't have any CDs with me and I don't fancy listening to the BBC world service for the next few hours so it looks like we are talking about the weather again.

My friends from the Teesside Walk and Talk Society (yes there is an acronym for that; and yes; it really is what you think!) are all petrol heads. It's a small group of just six and had I not been here I might have been with them in Norway this week on a Supercar Ice Driving experience. I have been following their adventure and I doubt they would admit it, but their Porsches look even less comfortable than this little thing.

They are basically hollowed out to allow the safety cages to be fitted. On the plus side the frozen lake they are on has rather fewer obstacles to content with than the roads here, but more of that later. I am not a big car fan but I can't help chuckling to myself and thinking we should get one of these and try it at home this winter.

The forty-five-minute journey to the car rental depot was only an appetiser for us today, gently easing us into a new chapter in our travels.

There is at least a five-hour drive to the Cameron Highlands ahead of us. KLIA is rather inconveniently situated to the south of the city. There is no easy way to get to our destination from here so there is no option but to head back to Kuala Lumpur and hope that when we get out the other side, that it will be easy enough to find the main highway North towards Ipoh.

Today is the last day of the long weekend holiday and the traffic back into the city is once again becoming rather heavy.

Melissa had warned us that it would be better to stick to the toll roads where possible because they were much better maintained and she had also recommended that we get a 'Touch and Go' card at the first toll booth we passed.

"Go to the very left-hand booth" she had said, "it costs ten Ringgit for the card, then they will load it up for you to whatever level you want. I don't normally drive as far as Penang but I guess that the tolls maybe forty or fifty Ringgit in total."

As it turned out she was spot on …… again. At the first booth I handed over one hundred Ringgit and left with both a new card and sense of optimism that we were starting to understand the place a little better.

My optimism was not matched by the weather. The clouds above us are dark grey for as far as the eye can see and we are gradually surrounded on both sides by riders on small motorbikes, wearing their jackets back to front. They travel with us for just a little while until they are forced to take shelter under the next bridge.

The first few miles are quite terrifying but I console myself with thoughts of John screaming his head off as he hurtles through the snow and ice in Norway and somehow it doesn't seem so bad after all.

The drive through the city centre is predictably slow but eventually we do see the signs for Ipoh and as we start to head out of the city once again, the flow of the traffic changes. Pretty soon almost all of the traffic is on the other carriageway heading south.

Half an hour later the rain is belting down so fast the windscreen wipers can hardly clear the water. Thankfully the drivers are sensible and the traffic heading north slows but the southbound carriage is now at a complete standstill with the traffic backed up for miles.

Eventually the rain eases allowing us to pick up the pace a little but it never really stops and as we pass over them, the engorged rivers seem to be filled with millions of gallons of coffee rather than rainwater.

There is a long way today go so we decide to press on as for long as it is practical given the conditions. The service stations are all chock full and apart from slowing down to pass through the fairly frequent tolls, getting ever slicker with the Touch and Go Card terminals, we are on the road for almost five hours straight before eventually turning off the main highway North near the small town of Tapah where we take a break for a coffee and a quick snack.

Distance wise our journey is almost over but from here we will be climbing up into the highlands on roads that twist and turn which means that the last forty miles or so up to Tanah Rata is going to take us at least another couple of hours.

As expected, when we set off again the drive is much slower but it also starts to get more interesting as we make our way through the beginnings of the rainforest. There are some dwellings here in the traditional style but mostly there are the odd huts and small platforms that I assume may be bus stops which allow people to wait without having to sit on the ground.

About a quarter of the way up we see the very picturesque Lata Iskandar Waterfall where the locals are bathing in the cool water and the tourists have stopped to take photos. This place has become something of an institution. Running along the road for about a quarter of a mile there are numerous shacks selling everything from rambutans and durian fruit to carved statues, even hardwood tables and chairs.

We have been here once before, many years ago. It is

a nice place to stop for a while and this time we don't have to worry about three children navigating the constant stream of traffic or the inevitable hazards that the water offers those too curious for their own good.

The road is very twisty though and space is very limited here. The rock face on the left is hard and unyielding whilst the gutters and shops on the right soon give way to a deep valley behind them, making both sides of the road equally treacherous.

Those heading uphill drive slowly out of necessity; but those coming down, including the coaches and lorries; are not so forgiving of the parked cars in their way.

I let Sue out first then pull over as close to the cliff face as I can get, but when I get out and see how close the traffic is I notice a few people moving on leaving larger spaces available so I decide to move it.

As I sit waiting for a gap in the traffic a lorry nearly takes the wing mirror off and I have visions of the liability on my credit card accelerating like the reels of a slot machine for the excess on the car. Fortunately, I manage to piece the wing mirror back together and it looks almost as good as new…… as long as you don't touch it.

When I catch up with her, Sue is oblivious to the drama. She is perusing everything the little shacks have to offer and clearly, I am not the only one who is now tired.

"I am looking for a blow pipe" she said.

"Pardon me?"

"A blow pipe, cousin Nev said we can get a blow pipe here and we can go into the jungle to see the fireflies".

"That's not a blow pipe you have hold of, that is wooden flute, and you hate the jungle because you get eaten alive"

"Good point, let's just grab a coke".

"Good idea."

"I am going to have a word with Nev when I get home."

Eventually we reach the town of Tanah Rata and what could be described as the 'plateau' where the highlands level out a bit and we are almost five thousand feet above sea level. The Cameron Highlands has the distinction of being the highest place in the Malay peninsula that is accessible by car and to be fair our little car had gotten us here safely but driving it up here was an exhausting experience.

It is getting late and the clouds have returned so we continue a few miles to a sharp bend in the road where we take a right turn and pull into the car park for our hotel, The Smoke House.

After checking in I slump down on the bed, connect to the WIFI and there is a message from Mr Gan.

He has been worrying about us all day and is checking up to make sure we arrived safely. How cool are Malaysian taxi drivers. They shuttle you around, act as tour guides, make alternative arrangements if they can't help you and then follow up to make sure you're ok.

Legends!

AN ENGLAND LONG FORGOTTEN

The Cameron Highlands covers almost three hundred square miles and the area was named in honour of the colonial government explorer and geographer William Cameron who surveyed the area in 1885.

Technically the area is known as a 'tableland' and in the 1920s and 1930s it started to be developed both for its agricultural potential and as a tourist destination.

The land is incredibly rich here and it is one of the places that the aboriginal Malay people, the 'Orang Asli' still live in the rainforest, but more about them later.

These are not the only highlands here in Malaysia, the Genting Highlands near Kuala Lumpur and the Lojing Highlands to the East being others of note. What they all have in common is the noticeably cooler temperature and lower humidity that make them attractive destinations to escape to when the heat becomes oppressive.

If you add a little cloud in to the equation as we currently have, then the daytime temperature falls to the mid-sixties Fahrenheit, making it not dissimilar to a late spring or an early summer day in England.

The Smoke House Hotel has something of an iconic

status in these parts. It looks like an old Tudor Manor House and if not for the exotic plants in the beautiful gardens it could easily remind one of the lake District in England, which of course was the idea.

The homesick colonials would have made this place their own from the 1930's until Malay independence in 1957. It is famous for serving tea and scones with clotted cream, as well as British style pies and cooked breakfasts.

This is one of the places Sue visited as a child so as her parents had done many years before we had decided to stay up here for a few days respite from the heat and to treat ourselves to a suite.

It sounds idyllic, and perhaps once it was, but its heyday has long since passed and it is in desperate need of investment.

Every window in the place is constantly open and it can at times feel very cold and draughty. The old metal window frames are rotting in places, many of the handles have snapped off and the floor coverings no longer have either colour or texture.

The dinner portions are enormous although not cheap and after dinner we retire to the bar before bed where the barman kindly lights a log fire in the open stone fireplace and Sue sits and chats with him, comparing their experience of growing up in Ipoh. It passes a few pleasant hours and evokes memories of a Malaysia long ago that we are looking forward to getting much closer to in the coming weeks.

The Warwick suite is now more reminiscent of an old nursing home than either an English Manor house or a hotel charging five-star prices, but in spite of its shortcoming the bed is very comfortable and combined with the much lower temperature at this altitude we do sleep well here.

We rise early as usual and breakfast is served in the conservatory. The windows are still open, perhaps they have been all night. Our waiter is wearing his hotel issue dress, over the top of which he is also wearing a combat jacket and gloves.

The menu once again is English themed and I give the full English breakfast a whirl. The are no real pork sausages or black pudding here, the bacon is 'beef' and more like jerky, the beans and mushrooms are at best lukewarm, and the fried egg is 'snotty' on top.

This may seem like quite a long list of minor whinges, which I suppose it is, but I had really been looking forward to staying here and it was much pricier than almost all of the other places we have stayed.

The people as always are the best part of our stay and the overall impression I am left with is of a theme park. It is as if it was once a true reflection of a faraway England but gradually each of the people who knew from direct experience what that was really like, had died or moved on and it is now being slowly diluted.

It is perhaps what a Chinese person who has never been to England thinks it is really like. A bit like a Disney version of America that people who have seen the movies expect to see when they go on holiday and of course real life is nothing like that.

Despite everything it does retain its iconic status here, there is always a steady stream of tourists, mainly oriental, who seem to relish sitting in the garden, drinking tea, and eating scones or dainty sandwiches almost from dawn until dusk.

It is also very well situated just off the main road between the two main towns of Tanah Rata and Brinchang which is helpful because we need to find a Dobi (laundry) soon.

Our first option at Tanah Rata looks fine on the outside but it is not what we are looking for. It turns out to be a self-service laundry and we really want to leave the washing then pick it up later when it is done, so we decide to head for the Boh Tea plantation a few miles away instead.

On the way we pass through Brinchang which at first glance is a real dump. The blocks of grey flats with balconies covered in brightly coloured clothes drying in the cool air look like they should be hanging off the side of a cliff face somewhere in the Himalayas.

In spite of that, unlike the hotel this is not a disappointment, this is the real life, this is what we have come to see and I make a mental note to stop here on the way back.

The most famous product from this area must be Cameron Tea and the Boh tea plantation is the most famous in Malaysia. The British found that the soil and climate here were well suited to their favourite tipple which they had long since developed a taste for during the days of the Indian Raj.

This place is well worth a visit. Even though it is not currently possible to tour the old factory where the leaves are processed into loose tea or teabags, to see the fields where this beverage, that we take for granted every day comes from, is a real education.

The slopes are so steep it is not surprising that even today it remains a manually intensive operation. You can walk through the bushes and take a tip from the plant. They are a deep green with a slightly waxy surface which gives them a bitter taste. Once, the workers would walk between the bushes pulling off only the top few leaves by hand and throwing them over their shoulders into large baskets.

The workers still live on the plantation in large wooden houses. Although they are now on two floors they still look more like huts. Only the small concrete school house seems like a concession to the 21st Century.

Mechanisation, such as it is, consists of a sort of lawnmower that is oblong shaped, about four feet long and three feet wide, which is held in the air above the plant and the trimmed leaves are caught in a net sack. They are then gathered by truck and brought up to the processing plant.

In the café, sitting on the balcony overlooking the acres of green fields, watching the workers harvest another crop we sip our loose-leaf tea and I eat a delicious cheesecake. Sue is also eating cheesecake and I have no idea how but somehow her cheesecake has been made with noodles?

I can't help marvelling at the contrast between this culture and home. It's not just the food.

How wonderful is it that one can sip a drink made from the tips of a bush that grows eight thousand miles away, on slopes so steep that many a fat European would have a heart attack just walking up them.

How little thought, if any, most people ever give to where something we put into our bodies every day comes from.

How hard they are working here; how lazy and complacent we have become and then my mind wanders. I lose the thread and wonder who on earth figured out you could make cheesecake with noodles?

As we make our way back out of the valley, thankfully once again all of the traffic is flowing in the opposite direction, it is heading for Kea farm market which seems to be the main market in this area selling a fantastic array of fresh fruit and vegetables.

These high roads are not somewhere you want to get stuck and soon it is relief to be in Brinchang again. We drive around to see if we can find a Dobi here. Luckily there is one opposite the car park, the 'Kedi Dobi' which proudly shouts the word 'Laundry' from a big blue and white sign with a picture of a washing machine next to it. The drama was completely unnecessary …we know what a Dobi is; but hey ho.

They promise they can do the washing for us and that we can have it back at 1pm tomorrow so the bargain is struck. We are hungry now but I can't find anywhere to pay for the parking. The Dobi owner tells us not to worry as the meter maids only come around in the morning. He is certain that they won't come back again today, so we leave the car and walk round to the high street to find a restaurant.

You must understand that I am using the word 'restaurant' in its widest possible sense here. Most of the places look like a garage lock up where they open the door and some little old lady is going hell for leather, stir frying noodles on a couple of gas burners. There is a drum of rice in the corner, a fridge filled with drinks and the younger women are collecting the plastic cups and plates in a bucket for the washing up.

No Michelin stars, no AA Rosettes, no food hygiene ratings, no good food guides, so you have to trust your judgement. The best advice is always to go where the locals go. Usually if a place is bouncing, there is a good reason for it.

In Brinchang, that place is the 'Delicious and Happiness Kitchen' no less. Unfortunately, that one is already full and there is a long queue so we make a mental note to return tomorrow. I remind myself that I should not be too disappointed. We have done well with the traffic, with finding the laundry and haven't paid for parking so our luck had to break at some point I suppose.

With a weary resignation the only option is to head to Tanah Rata and try our luck there.

First however we need petrol and once again I find myself indebted to Melissa.

"Use the cheapest petrol" she had said. "Don't pay for 98 Ron Octane, 95 is fine".

"She was right" I thought, as I scanned the pump prices.

It is about a third as much again for 98 Ron Octane which is a big difference, but after I have paid for the petrol, I was laughing to myself. I had paid about 42p a litre which is less than a third of the price at home. That put the smile back on my face and gave me a renewed sense of optimism for what the rest of the day might have in store.

TANAH RATA BINGO

Tanah Rata can probably lay claim to being the prettiest little town in this area where the main road through the highlands also serves as the long high street for the town.

Although tourists provide the main income stream for most of the shops, it is by no means a polished holiday destination. This is also a hub for the local community but even so, it is clear that the lack of tourists over the last two years has really taken its toll. The town also appears to be a popular destination for backpackers evidenced by the many cheap hostels that are advertised here and there.

We park up again and I have a dilemma. I still can't figure out how to pay for the parking and, if the parking wardens had already been to Brinchang I was wondering "where are they now?"

Once again, a friendly taxi driver comes to the rescue. He has seen me wandering around for nearly ten minutes and asks what the problem is so I explain our predicament.

"No problem" he said. "You get a book of parking tickets."

Now in my defence nowhere does it say you need a book of parking tickets.

"Where would I get one of those?" I asked hopefully.

He points across the road and says, "Every shop sells

them."

"Thank you."

Suddenly a light comes on in my head and I think "oh it's like a parking disc!" and head off across the road.

Five minutes later I realise that no, it isn't like a parking disc at all. It is a book of ten tickets that costs 6 ringgits, which is about £1.20, and they are best described a cross between bingo cards and scratch cards. 'What the hell do I do with these?'

First, in the top section you scratch off the year and, helpfully there are three to choose from. Then in the middle section you scratch off the month, then a day of the week and in the final section you pick the time AM, PM, hours, and minutes.

So far so good, but then it gets complicated. I want to stay for more than one hour so do I scratch off the times sequentially or all the same time? And if I put two out with the same time on and they are both for an hour what happens?

It seems like an awful lot of effort to pay 28p to park.

In the end Sue is getting bored, hungry, and losing the will to live so we just wing it.

By the time I am finished I too am exhausted by the whole process to care so we head back across to the line of shops across the road and amble past a restaurant called 'Restoran Sri Brinchang.'

A bearded man with an orange cap, who is presumably the owner, is standing outside like a hunter looking for passing tourists. He is a real professional, a seasoned veteran. Seeing the blank and mentally exhausted look on my face, he immediately recognises his opportunity and springs his trap.

Looking at our necklaces and bracelets he asks, "have you been to India?"

I can't help thinking that this is a ploy to catch us off guard. Then before we realise what is happening, Sue has been dragged inside to look at all the food and any will power she may have is out of the window.

I would estimate that it took less than two minutes for us to be sitting at a table with two plastic trays of delicacies ladled up from an array of vats, heated up in the microwave then served with warm naan and a side order of tandoori Chicken.

It was excellent value too, around £5.00 including bottles of water for both of us and it was really tasty so once again I am enamoured of the Southern Indian culture.

Feeling better, we set out to explore the town which seems to be a lot larger than I remember from our last visit here. There are quite lot of small hotels, hostels, and apartments for rent here, and a small 1970's style, boxy but wholly uninteresting shopping centre, set back from the high street.

It looks like they are preparing for a weekend night market too with steel frames and wooden platforms left in the market square behind the car park. A few small vans are already parked up. My guess is that the traders are sleeping in them as well as using them for transporting their wares. It is a shame that we are going to miss it.

In the general store along the street I want some snacks for the room, some nuts perhaps to snack on while I watch TV later and some for the car, some boiled sweets to help me concentrate on the twisty roads when we leave the highlands.

I can't help noticing that everything up here that is in a sealed plastic bag looks like it is about to explode. The bags were presumably packed down in the lowlands and the lower pressure up here is clearly visible in the bulging packets. It really hits home how high we are.

It is getting dark now and some of the shops are starting to close but on the upper level of the shopping centre, looking out over the street I can see there are quite a few coffee shops so we take advantage before heading back to the hotel.

Later that evening sitting by the fire back in the hotel we hear English voices behind us.

A couple have seen us sitting by the fire and were about to leave to find somewhere else to shelter from the draught blowing in, but we invited them to join us. Sergei and Jane have travelled up from Ipoh today and it turns out they are from Cumbria. Well Sergei isn't, he's from Russia but he works in IT for the council in Carlisle.

Seeing the various bits of cheap tat, that we acquired at the Caves of Batu Jane asks, "Have you been to India?"

Blimey this is becoming a bit of a theme. I don't

know why I am surprised. To me the necklaces just look like shrivelled walnuts on a piece of string, but I suppose that to anyone familiar with the symbology they would be as recognisable as the crucifix I am also wearing.

It turns out that our new friends have travelled extensively in India and make some interesting recommendations should we decide to become a bit more adventurous.

We pass a pleasant couple of hours in conversation and then head off to bed.

The next morning, our aim is to head to Kea Farm Market which is on the far side of Brinchang. That works well as we can grab our clothes from the Dobi on the way back later in the afternoon. This is our final day here and there are a few things that need to be sorted out ahead of the long journey to Penang tomorrow because that is going to be a long day and another early start will be necessary.

The market is a sprawling affair which straddles across both sides of the main road. In a nod to health and safety there is a makeshift carpark, some plastic road barriers to prevent cars making U turns if they miss the entrance and what I would very loosely call a pedestrian crossing, or a target for drivers to aim for depending on your point of view. Trust me, up here both are equally valid.

The Pasar Pagi Kea Farm Market to give it its full name, is the largest in the area and there is an incredible variety of produce here. Some of it comes from farms as you would expect but a lot of it comes straight from the rain forest and if you like exotic ingredients then you will not be disappointed.

Rambutans, water apples, various kinds of sweet potatoes, okra, gai choy, brinjal, pineapples, raw sugar cane, palm leaves, lychees, snake fruit, papaya, pomelos, coconuts and the vegetarian's favourite, Jackfruit. You name it, they have it, as well as things you probably can't put a name to.

I am almost sorry that there are no cooking facilities in our hotel room. It is making me hungry just looking at it all and there is a scent in the air of warm chestnuts roasting in what look like metal bin lids. I grab a small bag for 1 ringgit (20p) and start eating the contents with a toothpick, only to find out that they are not chestnuts at all.

To my surprise they are in fact a variety of purple sweet potato but honestly if I closed my eyes, I would struggle to tell the difference. I resist the temptation to close my eyes however as I have no desire to get run over.

There is also of course the much-revered durian fruit. This one I really cannot get my head around but it is ever present in Malaysia.

They grow about four hundred and fifty thousand tons of this fruit every year and it has numerous uses. They make drinks with it, ice creams, it is a key ingredient in lots of dishes here, but it smells like rotting flesh, it is so awful that it is not permitted in hotels and it is actually illegal to take it on public transport in Thailand, Singapore, or Hong Kong.

On the valley side, where the land drops away there is a hotel with a children's playground inside, as well as a sheep sanctuary of all things. I am surprised by this discovery on two counts. Firstly because it seems to be loosely modelled on a Wallace and Gromit cartoon and secondly because we have not seen a single sheep anywhere in Malaysia yet.

Continuing down the hill there is also a large food hall. It is still quite early but I can hear the roar of the gas burners as they are heating the oil in the large woks and preparing snacks to go on skewers.

The shape of these snacks is not at all familiar and they look black, but not burnt, and I can't quite put my finger on what they are. Eventually, I come to the conclusion that they are in fact cuttlefish……hmmm …. cuttlefish on a stick, the colour probably comes from the ink they produce.

One mystery solved already today and I am feeling like Thelma from Scooby Doo so I suggest quitting while we are ahead and making our way to Brinchang to pick up our washing. Unfortunately, the Dobi has not finished with our washing yet, so we decide to take a closer look at the town, wandering around aimlessly to see what more it has to offer.

At the bottom of the hill, we come across the rather hilariously named Hotel Tittiwangsa. The double-entendres here are the gift that keeps on giving. My Chinese isn't that good but I am keen to try everything while I am here.

From the back of the hotel, I can see a Temple perhaps a quarter of a mile away across the valley. This is the

Sam Poh Buddhist Temple which is the largest in the area. I can't see an obvious way to it but Google Maps shows a road leading there so I figure the best thing to do is to drive and we return to the car.

I figured wrong, soon we are in a campsite in the middle of the jungle and although I reason that it is probably not far away, the Temple is not visible at all now.

It is in all likelihood possible to get to it on foot from here as there are designated walkways, but to be honest it's hot, it's humid and neither of us fancies being eaten alive. Also judging by the entrance to the campsite it looks more like a set from the film Deliverance. I am worried we are going to come across a cross eyed kid playing a banjo who only communicates through his music ….and I don't have a guitar with me so that is not going to work.

God only knows how, but channelling my inner Thelma once again, we did eventually find the Temple. The scale of the place was quite impressive, and the giant golden statues that seem to scowl down at visitors are awesome, but it turned out to be slightly disappointing overall.

I am in search of history and age-old wisdom to sooth my troubled mind. This is no ancient relic though, it was in fact built in 1976 while Abba was busy belting out Dancing Queen, and in some places, it still seems to be under construction.

Most of the building seems to be either a school, monks' quarters, or kitchens where the staff were busy preparing meals for a steady stream of other visitors who clearly had not been traumatised by the jungle but had simply walked down the now visible path from Brinchang.

It did however fill a couple of hours and left us hungry so we chanced our arm once again to see if you could get a table in the 'Delicious and Happiness Kitchen.' Fortunately, we manged to get the last small table tucked away by the fridge which gave us the chance to see why it was so popular.

It was still early and they had already run out of some of the favourites but the food was superb and it was impossible not to stare at the tables around us; where large families were ordering numerous colourful dishes, laden with everything the menu still had to offer.

Pretty soon both of us are stuffed. I have just eaten more ginger and green chillies on a single plate than you can shake a stick at, and we are determined that the afternoon is going to have a slower pace to it. We retrieve our belongings from the Dobi, take them back to the hotel to rest for a few hours before we start to pack for our journey tomorrow, then we head back to Tanah Rata for a last look around the town.

I manage to swerve the guy standing outside the 'Restoran Sri Brinchang' this time but he smiles anyway and says hello as we pass on by.

Today I just want to try one of the coffee shops we had seen before on the balcony of the shopping centre called 'Naux Pastry Café.'

Pastry isn't something I would associate with Malaysia but I had been intrigued by all of the certificates on the wall and two ceramic plates which take pride of place on the counter celebrating the skill of Goh Boon Xia.

Below the trophies, in the display there is a selection of delicate cakes that would give any Parisian or Austrian Café a run for their money. It is Goh's mother who serves us whilst his father is doing the washing up in the kitchen. Although the whole place is tiny, she explains that everything is hand made on the premises.

This place is a real gem and so unexpected. I don't know why it should be, people the world over tend to be very innovative in what they eat and how they use the ingredients they have available to them, but the richness of the food here continues to surprise me.

All that remains now of our time in the highlands is to spend a final night by the open fire and a few hours to take stock of the people we have met and the things we have experienced.

Upon our return, it is a pleasant surprise to find that the fire is already lit, but unfortunately it is surrounded by a large group of Germans who are here for dinner!

SNOTTY EGGS AND ROAD WARRIORS

Today we have a long drive to Penang which will take up most of the day and we set out first for the city of Ipoh.

On this first leg we will be retracing our steps through Brinchang and beyond before turning left onto Route 185 to begin the long descent from the highlands.

The further we explore in the highlands the more life we seem to find.

The improvised market stalls are everywhere along the road. Combined with the poly tunnels spread across the flatter areas they bring back distant memories of Blue Peter where everything was made with plastic, string, and various bits of household rubbish.

Here in the mountains the whole economy seems to be built that way, but it is just a conduit for the riches of the rainforest to get to the bellies of the people.

Once the descent begins in earnest a truly magnificent panoramic vista opens up before us. Miles upon miles of hillside, covered in tropical rainforest spread out into the distance as far as the eye can see and beyond. As you look further towards the horizon the view does not end, it just seems to get slightly hazier, the ridges seem somehow less defined giving the impression that the rain forest is endless.

I would like more time to enjoy the view. It is breath taking so I am very grateful when we come to an enforced stop due to road works giving us a chance to get out of the car and to just soak it up for a few more minutes. Travelling through the forest for mile after mile refreshes the soul and you cannot help but feel connected to nature here, to a much grander universe.

I have no doubt that God has a sense of humour and is keen to show us where we are going wrong. That is reaffirmed when we eventually get to the outskirts of Ipoh where my first impression is that they either forgot to finish building it, or it has recently been condemned and they have not quite finished dismantling it. What a contrast in so short a time.

This is not our time to explore Ipoh really. The plan is to come back this way next week. Today is just a lunch stop so we make our way as best we can to the central area and park up so that we can visit a highly recommended restaurant called the Durbar at FMS.

'Kung Hei Fat Choi' means wishing you happiness and prosperity if you are Cantonese or 'Gong Xi Fa Cai' in mandarin which is what the signs everywhere here seem to say

We have seen it everywhere but here it seems to have more meaning for Sue, as this is the main town in the area she lived as a child, in a suburb called Batu Gajah, which means Elephant Rock or Stone Elephant.

Much of Ipoh's road system is one way, and it proves a little tricky at first to get near to our target but eventually, I manage to get parked in what is either a small private car park or a public park where someone is just collecting money at the gate because they can.

Anyway, it does the trick and we find the restaurant about a hundred yards away, situated in a beautiful old colonial style building overlooking what I presume was once a cricket pitch.

We are very fortunate to get a table here today, it is often booked weeks in advance and they are currently fully booked for the rest of the month, but when we chat to the lovely lady on the desk and explain our pilgrimage, she manages to find us a table on condition that we must hand it back in two hours. On a different day that might be a problem but today it's fine.

The Durbar was established in 1906 giving it a claim to being the oldest Chinese restaurant in Malaysia. It is quite famous, and the reviews on Trip Advisor are excellent so we are really looking forward to this experience.

The restaurant is spotlessly clean. The décor inside has a Chinese twist with the usual red lanterns, ornate black lacquered panels, and tropical plants but it also pays homage to its colonial past with tiled floors, extravagant stately home style coving and ceiling fans.

The walls are covered with framed newspaper cuttings of horse racing, cricket and news relating to the British Royal Family. There are portraits of Queen Elizabeth II and King Charles III too, leaving me wondering what they will make of the coming coronation of the new King later this year.

The lady takes our order and passes it on before returning to tell us more about the history of the place. Apparently upstairs there is something of a museum, unfortunately it is closed now but it is worth noting for when we return.

Chinese food here bears little resemblance to what we are used to at home. The side dishes of chips and various dips are familiar enough but the main dishes are where you really notice it. One dish is a type of sticky rice with prawn crackers and some battered chicken on the bone, topped with a fried egg. Almost all meat here, regardless of what it is or where you eat is served 'on the bone.'

The other dish is harder to describe, although it is a favourite of the local Chinese and reminds Sue of her childhood, it makes me want to baulk. It contains noodles, chicken, prawns, mushrooms, and pak choi which are fine, but I had not realised that the 'egg gravy' was basically just a few raw eggs thrown into the mixture.

The only way I can describe it would be like a 'snotty egg' dip. Now there is nothing wrong with eating raw eggs and to the Eastern palate this is a delicacy but it is not for me.

Strangely it is not so much the taste but more the sensation of the slime rolling around my teeth and gums that I don't like. I am only too pleased when I can order a black coffee to take the sensation away but I am less pleased a little later when it fails to settle my stomach resulting in a close encounter with the, albeit immaculate, squat toilet that is lurking behind a very large parlour palm to the rear of the bar.

All in all, a very interesting experience but not one I care to repeat. The restaurant is fabulous but I will have to exercise a little more care in ordering on my next visit. For now, it is time to resume our journey, navigating the one-way system again on to what looks like a main through road and to find the main road North to Penang.

The drive north from Ipoh is spectacular.

As you leave the city the road climbs over the mountains then it dips down the other side where suddenly the road is the only thing left of mankind and you are once again completely surrounded by mountains and rain forest.

The traffic heading south is bonkers. Penang is a major centre for Chinese culture in Malaysia and clearly a lot of people are still making their way back to Kuala Lumpur after celebrating Chinese New Year.

Although we are still travelling north against the flow, it is still necessary to concentrate as the road changes from two to three lanes, and then back again.

Just to make it more interesting the motorbikes are also playing their deadly game of cat and mouse, weaving in and out of the traffic from both sides.Suddenly we find ourselves in the midst of a group of perhaps twenty, some with solo riders, others with pillion passengers and some with children or even furniture onboard.

They do wear crash helmets here but the rest of the 'safety' gear seems to consist of flip flops, loose trousers, paired with short sleeve shirts, or if they are really safety conscious, long sleeve shirts for added protection.

Up ahead I can see the dark clouds gathering. Within moments the car is engulfed in torrential rain and once again we seem to be gliding along a river rather than driving on a main road.

I have to remember that nothing is automatic in the car. I am frantically trying to get the lights to shine brighter and the windscreen wipers to go faster but there is no choice other than to slow down to a crawl.

I am worried about colliding with a motorcycle but they have all miraculously disappeared. As we travel under a road bridge, we can see that they have taken shelter underneath. The sudden downpours can be very heavy so for safety this is a thing here and there are signs on many bridges indicating that they should do this.

Gradually the rain clears and I can see by the roadside a few riders, with their hazard lights still flashing. They are retrieving jackets from under their seats and putting them on backwards. Then mere moments later they are once again weaving their way in and out of the traffic playing their deadly game.

We are grateful to be in a car but we know that the riders outside will be dry in a few minutes too. Riding at sixty miles an hour in the airstream of near 100-degree heat must be like riding into a giant hair dryer.

Things soon settle down again allowing us to pay more attention to our surroundings once more. Traveling northwards, gradually the forest becomes more mixed and dotted with palm and rubber plantations. Eventually the closer you get to Butterworth, the main town opposite Penang Island; the forest disappears altogether and both sides of the road consist of just mile after mile of plantations.

These two products, and their versatility, were partly the reason that Malaysia was strategically important to the British Empire and also why it became a prime target for the Japanese in the 1940s.

The Palm plantations tend to be large scale whereas the Rubber plantations seem to be much smaller but both remain vital economic resources for Malaysia. Although many rubber products have gradually been replaced by plastic alternatives over the last 30 years the natural product has a number of advantages, not least because it is, under proper conditions, a naturally bio-degradable product.

There are over one million hectares of land used for Rubber production here which contribute almost half of the world's rubber. The rubber industry is worth £4Bn per annum and has been as high as three times that historically, but it is Palm oil that is the big earner.

The Malaysian Palm oil industry is worth a staggering £17Bn, which equates to two and half percent of Malaysia's GDP. It is the second biggest producer in the world, producing almost twenty times more than the third biggest producer, Guatemala, and only Indonesia produces more.

Palm oil is the most widely used vegetable oil in the world and this versatile product is used in everything from cosmetics, to soap, shampoo, cleaning products, it can even be used as a biofuel. More than five and three quarter million hectares of land are turned over for its production.

These figures are mind blowing and I am not surprised that a high priority is given to them, but I cannot help but compare the plantations to the incredible richness of the forests that have been cleared to create them. How much biodiversity has been lost, how many birds, reptiles, insects, and mammals?

When I think back just a couple of days to the things that we tried at Kea Market in the highlands, where the forest produce still dominates, I could literally cry.

Even though the plantations themselves look quite green and lush to western eyes and there are cattle wandering between the trees, when you add in the soil erosion, the carbon emission to the atmosphere and the water pollution they also contribute to, this is truly a paradise lost.

Thankfully as we near Butterworth and the Penang Bridge, the clouds clear, allowing us the opportunity to enjoy the last rays of the afternoon sun before it disappears behind Penang Hill in the West. The high-rise buildings of Penang Island beyond are also now clearly visible, which all helps to bring a sense of relief and to lighten the mood.

GEORGETOWN

It seems like it has been a very long journey and it has. It is not the just time aspect, but also being physically cooped up in the car, concentrating for so long. Now however, we seem to be a world away from the highlands; even though I can still just about make them out in my rear-view mirror.

If nature makes her statements with the forest covered mountains behind us behind, then man has been determined to make his mark here in front of us.

Once you pass through the toll barriers, you start to appreciate what a marvel of engineering the Penang Road bridge is. It is a low level bridge that glides just above the water for over four miles. It is a spectacular way to greet our destination and soon we are on the island heading for the historic capital, Georgetown.

For the final time today, we are grateful to be heading in the opposite direction to everyone else as a car crash on the other carriageway has brought the traffic to a standstill.

According to Wikipedia, Penang has a population of around three quarters of a million people. Here on the island at least, sixty five percent of them are ethnic Chinese and only twenty one percent are ethnic Malays, with various other groups such as Indians (particularly Tamils), Thais, Europeans etc making up the balance. Almost a quarter of the population live in the historical core of the city, covering an area of just seven square miles which makes it one of the most densely populated urban areas in Asia.

I am always a bit suspicious of the accuracy of 'facts' that anyone can contribute to, but it doesn't really matter. You get the idea, it's big, it's busy and it's different to the rest of Malaysia.

It feels like a bit of an understatement but with its many different districts, Georgetown is both a bustling modern metropolis and a racial melting pot with a rich and complex history. The Chinese influences are immediately more visible here, and we are relishing the opportunity to explore them later but we are not out of the woods yet in terms of the traffic and I must first concentrate on finding our hotel.

The six lanes of traffic are 'stop start' for the last few miles, and the closer you get to the old town the more erratic the combined 'traffic' seems to be.

There are colourful shops and makeshift stalls lining the road and here it is not just the motorcycles and cars we need to watch out for, there are also cyclists and the lack of footpaths means that there are pedestrians wandering onto the carriageway too. To make matters worse the motorcycles are now travelling in both directions on the same side of the road.

I would laugh at the chaos around us but it's getting late and being tired the last thing I want is to 'clip' someone.

The sun is setting as we make our way down the colourful lantern lined streets, past Buddhist and Indian temples, until we finally pull into the carpark at the magnificent Eastern & Oriental Hotel. Our little red car has once again served its purpose with aplomb and it is almost with a sense of disbelief that, after all we have driven through and seen, we have not only arrived, but that we have done so without getting a scratch on it.

I am very relieved to be here. It feels like a real triumph and there is a sound track playing in my head, 'We are the Champions' by Queen.

Although I can't be certain, perhaps other road users have given us a little more latitude than you might have otherwise expected had the car been something bigger or more expensive. Whatever the reason I am grateful.

I don't know if this is actually a public car park or part of the hotel, or how much it costs and it is asking for a card to gain entry. To my surprise it seems to accept the 'Touch N Go' cards that we have been using for the toll roads. That will do, for now. I am tired so I will use that and figure out if I have enough credit on it to be able to leave when the time comes.

Situated right on the waterfront overlooking Butterworth on the mainland, this place has a special interest for us on this trip. The rooms are sumptuous with huge bathrooms, his and hers sinks, a giant roll top bath, a walk-in shower, queen sized beds, TV, desk, comfortable chairs, and a balcony that makes the most of the fabulous sea view.

Sue is beaming, her late mother and father did much of their courting in this hotel in the early 1950s at the tea dances that were a regular feature. This is something we are keen to explore, but first a much-needed shower, a cup of tea and quick nap.

Although it is tempting to stay in bed, the hunger pangs are getting the better of us both now. Sitting down for most of the day has done us no favours at all so to be honest a little bit of exercise would not go a miss.

We head out on foot and try to get our bearings. At the front of the hotel there are two very smart and friendly looking staff in uniform. They are wearing short sleeved shirts, short trousers with a brown belt, white socks, highly polished black oxford style shoes and colonial style pith helmets.

A bright red, open top Morgan two-seater sports car, contrasting against the pristine white of the hotel building really completes the very traditional facade. With the sea just in front of us and the palm trees swaying gently in the breeze you are instantly transported back to the 1950's.

On further examination I notice that the little sports car has a ribbon on it and there is a steady stream of luxury cars arriving which would seem to indicate a party of some sort is taking place. Sure enough, the large dining room looks very busy with rather smartly dressed families so we decide to head into town and make our way to the rear of the building and the main road. Rather than risk our lives crossing the busy roads the easiest thing is to follow it around to what appears to be a convent with a playing field next to it. The mind boggles but I will figure it out later.

Then we spot something very rare indeed in this part of the world, a pedestrian bridge across the road. By sheer co-incidence this takes us across to St Xavier's Institution, which is where Sue's brother, Peter, went to school way back in the 1960s. At some point we will come back here and learn more about it, but for now we just head down a lane which runs along the side of the school, between it and the very distinctive building, The Church of the Assumption.

When I see the street sign 'Love Lane' I can't help smiling and imagining a much more innocent time. A few minutes later we find ourselves on Chulia Street or Lebuh Chulia as it is known locally, which is one of the oldest roads in Georgetown.

It's not quite 'satay street' in Singapore; but there is a good selection of hawker stalls here and there is a steady stream of people coming to eat at them. Perhaps it is the time of the evening but it's not as busy as I had expected and there seems to be a little more going on just off the main drag in Carnarvon Street.

One stall in particular proves too difficult to resist. It looks as though it has been built on an axle with two pram wheels and it has five levels or shelves, each laden with things on skewers.

I recognise some of them as fish balls, chicken, prawns, vegetables, tofu, beef salami, crab sticks, but there are many more things I don't recognise.

At the front there are three large tin bowls of various spicy dips presumably chilli, peanut satay, and sambal. Then in front of those are two large metal vats, of what look like boiling water, but which are probably in fact filled with some sort of broth.

It is quite an ingenious contraption which presumably the owner simply pushes home when he or she is finished for the evening.

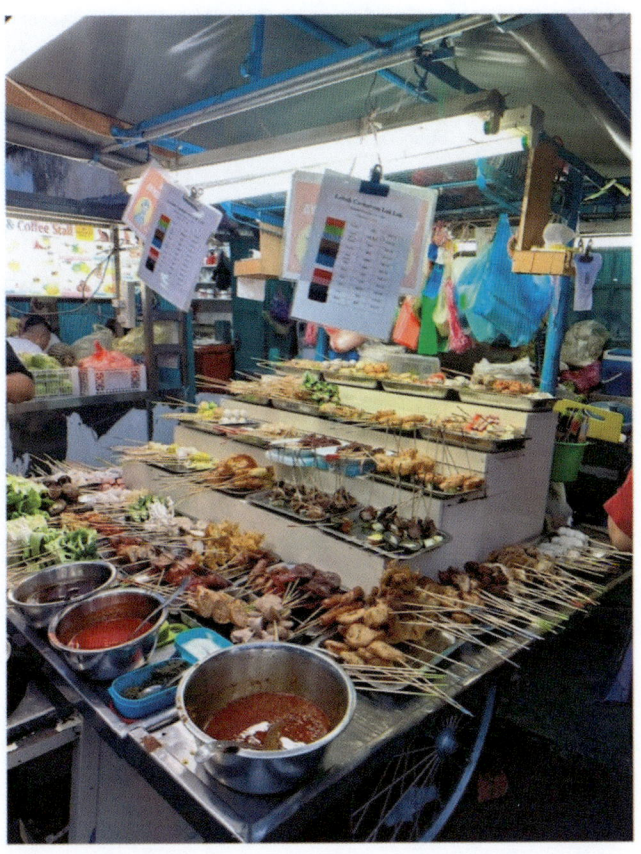

Behind the colourful display a middle-aged Chinese lady has been watching us and she leaves the two-foot-long charcoal strip on which she is cooking chicken and prawn satay sticks by the dozen. She steps over a deep gutter and hands us a couple of very well used menus. To be honest I am already pretty much set on what I can see cooking, the smell of the smoke infused with the juices from the meat is quite intoxicating so I just smile, point, and ask for two plates.

This seems to be a universal language here. She in turn smiles back then points to two small plastic chairs and a table just inside a small shop to the left of her stall. It is once again our turn to smile, before stepping over the two-foot-deep gutter, grabbing two bottles of water from the fridge on the way to the table, where we sit and wait for our evening meal.

It is simple and cheap but tasty and adequately filling. After our meal we decide to see what else is going on Carnarvon Street before making our way back to the hotel, albeit a via rather circuitous route.

I am not sure if I can manage a dessert but we scan the various shops and cafes nearby just in case, then we take the opportunity to wander down the length of Chulia street to the rather swanky looking George Hotel then onto the very exotic 'Chong Fatt Tse' or Blue Mansion Hotel.

It has been a very long day but we can already sense the promise of lots to explore in the coming days.

Breakfast is early as usual and the main dining room on the ground floor offers a great choice not unlike the Pan Pacific in Singapore. It is the best, and the largest, breakfast we have had in a while.

We noticed signs had already been set up in the reception announcing another wedding function, indeed there appears to be a steady stream of them throughout our visit here which just underpins how iconic this place is here.

The dining room is filling up rapidly, we're not the first in at six thirty AM and by seven o'clock it is bouncing so I am glad to get out. I suppose I should not be surprised; it is Saturday after all. Everyone else is probably looking forward to making the most of their day too.

For us that means getting to Penang Hill, ideally before everyone else has finished their breakfast, so we need to retrieve our little red chariot. I wasn't sure how much the parking cost or if would have enough credit on it to pay on the 'Touch N Go' card so I head to reception to see how we get out, and if it is possible to top up the card here.

To my surprise the concierge tells us he can validate the card so the parking will be free. He also adds that they are quite useful and some tourist attractions accept them as well but unfortunately "no", the Hotel cannot add credit to them. If I want to do that, I should top it up at the petrol station the next time I fill up. The more I discover about this place, the more I like it.

Although we can actually see Penang Hill in the distance there is a one-way element to the first part of the journey through the old part of Georgetown to negotiate. I thought the roads might be a little quieter given that it is the weekend. That was my first mistake.

I don't know the roads yet so I engage the sat nav and it soon becomes clear that it doesn't know the roads either. I have not seen a 'Tom Tom' for quite a few years which makes me think that this one has not been updated in at least a decade. Whilst it has been fine for the country roads and main highways where there are road signs to correlate to, in this dense urban environment it was going to be a very different game.

This is the 'school of life' and if I am not careful it could quite literally become the 'school of hard knocks.' Now the Queen soundtrack playing in my head is no longer 'We Are the Champions' it is the lyrics for 'Save Me' that I can hear.

Here beginneth the first lesson. I learn pretty quickly that 'Lebuh' is an avenue and 'Jalan' is a street, with the latter tending to be larger, busier, and more likely to be a through road.

I also learn that the voice on the sat nav talks too fast, can't pronounce the names properly, even the familiar names like McAllister, Queen, or Farquhar, and it is highly prone to asking me to turn left or right when I am in the midst of three lanes of traffic. As Sue will testify, I am not great with left and right at the best of times.

When you add into the equation the lack of pavements, huge gutters, and the mix of traffic, which this morning also includes dozens of Rickshaws then driving in Georgetown is something akin to the 'Whacky Races' and I have to say I love it.

The driving style here is 'positive' rather than 'aggressive' but it is a sort of game of nerves. No one wants to have an accident, especially with a cheap Proton Saga, but it's as though the Chinese cultural need to 'save face' extends to driving, and this means that they cannot give way until the very last second.

It really is very entertaining but eventually we reach the station at the bottom of the hill and we need to park up.

PENANG HILL

The name Penang Hill is actually a little confusing as there are several peaks here, but it is usually taken to signify the most developed one, which is more correctly called 'Bukit Bendera' in Malay or 'Flagstaff Hill.'

Access to Penang Hill itself is free but the challenge is getting to the top. One of the many things it is famous for is the funicular railway that takes you to the top in just over four minutes. We have been to Penang once before as a family but that was in 2010 and the railway was being refurbished.

Cars are not allowed on the Hill and although it is possible to walk to the top (this is the free part), that would be no mean feat in the constant thirty degree plus heat, so on that occasion we didn't take the opportunity to visit.

The station gets really busy. By 10.00 am we know it will be heaving so it is important to get there quite early. We buy two return tickets for the equivalent of about £14. I am surprised to note that there is a fast-track ticket too, but it is almost three times the price. I incorrectly assume that it is getting up to the top which will be the problem and it is fine now, so that won't be something we need to consider, but as the day wears on we are in for a surprise.

The train is full, but somehow by sheer fluke, I end up right at the front with an almost unobstructed view of the climb and what a journey it is.

Most funiculars are historical relics, often fixtures more associated with British seaside towns like Saltburn, Babbacombe, or Lynmouth where they were originally used to ferry bathers to and from the beach. Typically, the carriages are of wooden construction, of Victorian or Edwardian design, and they climb to a height of perhaps one or two hundred feet.

This one is much grander in both design and scale. It was originally opened to the public in 1923 but today it resembles a modern commuter train and whisks you up over two thousand feet. It is one of a kind in Malaysia, it can carry over a million visitors a year up and down the hill.

The only things reminiscent of the Victorians or Edwardians now are what look like cast iron street lights that line the track, and an old wooden carriage deliberately positioned on a short, now redundant section of track to the side of the line, about halfway up.

It is almost impossible to see the track itself until you are on it, as it is so well hidden by the rain forest and in places by rocks on either side, where the gap in between was presumably excavated for the line with dynamite.

The coolness of the air-conditioned carriage contrasts sharply with the humidity outside, and amazingly I can see a few brave souls looking very hot and bothered who are making the journey on foot, clambering up the steep paths that at times do run close to the track.

As if to emphasise how hard their climb is, the angle of our ascent seems impossibly steep. Near the top there is a tunnel which is believed to be the steepest in the world at almost 38 degrees. For comparison, the equivalent gradient on a road would make it virtually impossible to drive.

When we exit the station at the top and head for the viewing area, we are surprised to see that the queue for the train going down is already about three times longer than the queue was to come up the hill. Fortunately we won't have to worry about that for a few hours yet.

The air up here is a little cooler and although it is also

a little hazy due to the heat, the views are spectacular. It is not just what you can see from here, but there is also a lot up on the hill itself to see.

Our first diversion is perhaps surprisingly a Hindu Temple. Like the main temple at The Batu Caves. This one is also dedicated to Lord Murugan. Now that the blisters on my feet have cleared up, I am keen to go inside to take a closer look at the shrine.

From the front the building has the appearance of being supported by four main pillars. The two at the sides are multicoloured but not particularly ornate, but the two in the middle that support the portico and lead the eye inside, are carved with what appear to be hybrid human/elephant men, standing on two feet which end in claws like those of a reptile.

Above them along the roofline there are rows of male and female figures, some are green skinned and others have multiple arms or heads.

The whole building is painted every colour of the rainbow which somehow makes it seems to relish the stream of sunshine raining down upon it. It is as if it is drawing even more colour from the sky, knowing that even though we cannot see it in white light, that all the colours of the rainbow are still ever present.

This shrine is spotless inside and the marble tiles on the floor are a welcome cooling balm to my bare feet. In pride of place in the centre is another small shrine with a door guarded by two, four armed figures. Inside I can make out what appears to be a male figure seated on a throne covered with garlands of white, red, and yellow flowers with similar albeit smaller and presumably female figures, standing on either side of him.

At the front of the shrine there is small table with what look like offerings and in pride of place a replica of Murugan's heart shaped spear tip.

Almost next door, but a little higher on the hill presumably to make a, not so subtle, point, is a Muslim Mosque.

Whilst I am sure this Mosque is equally important and grand to those of the state religion, to the casual observer it is a much more conservative, severe, almost drab building by comparison.

I am making no judgement here; I merely share the impressions they seem to evoke. One seems to revel in the world, (and indeed all worlds) in all its forms, it is a riot of colour that leads towards contemplating everything, all at once, whilst the other seems to seek to remove all distraction to allow one to focus only on inner thoughts and vistas.

Two very different routes to what may ultimately be the same destination perhaps, who knows?

Nature has its own Temple here too. The 'Habitat' is a world class discovery site designed to help educate people and to let them experience the Malaysian rain forest first hand.

In fact, the whole of the wider 'Penang Hill' is designated by UNESCO as a biosphere reserve and looking over the adjacent forest covered hills it is not hard to see why. Entrance to the Habitat is quite expensive but it is for a good cause, it is also well worth it and it has a few surprises to offer.

There are guided tours that we can join here but we decide to just explore the nature walk under our own steam. Once you are amongst the trees at ground level the humidity in the air seems to increase to the point where it becomes almost visible and the soundtrack changes too.

Here in the jungles the voices are not those of people, they are the call of birds, the slithering of hidden things in the leaves below, the droplets of water running down the rock face dripping into small pools full of frogs, but above all they are the chattering of the insects, the crickets and cicadas that seem to relish the heat of the day.

It's not hard to imagine how quickly one could become lost in a rain forest with only a few feet of visibility in any direction and no clear sky to help navigate by either sun, moon, or stars. That's one of the reasons that we still know so little about what they contain but on the plus side it allows us to speculate about what treasures we may still one day discover in there.

In contrast the next section we encounter in the Habitat, called Langur way, is apparently the world's longest two-span, canopy walk and it is incredible to walk amongst the treetops. Here you feel closer to the sky and, through the tree tops, you get the first sense of just how far the forest really stretches.

When you can see the ground below you realise again how steep the hillsides are. The trees just seem to grow, arrow like, heading for the sunlight and many are well over a hundred feet tall.

It's getting towards noon now and although there are monkeys and many other species in the forest, they seem to be taking a nap.

The real jewel in the crown here has to be the steel framed viewing platform. From underneath as you approach, it appears like an arch overhead, much like the shape of a rainbow, but when you get up close you realise that it is actually a roughly egg-shaped construction.

The structure itself is not that high, perhaps only thirty feet or so, but combined with its situation on a small flat hill top, it is just high enough to lift the observer clear of the surrounding trees and the views from here are breath taking. I click to the right and to the left but I already know that no matter how many I take; the photographs are never going to do this place justice.

From here it is possible see various buildings which were previously hidden from view. We can see what would have once been the Governor's retreat in colonial days, along with a sanatorium of sorts. This was once where the European elite or favoured officials would be allowed to recuperate from diseases like cholera and dysentery which were rife in the town below.

Some of the buildings up here remain in government ownership but others have now been repurposed.

Set your gaze a little further south or west, and the rain forest seems to go on for miles. I can see branches swaying in the distance where troops of monkeys have at last come to life and are now patrolling their territories via the treetops.

However, it is to the North and the East that the views really give you a sense of perspective. They say that on a clear day you can see Langkawi from here, an island further north, close to the Malaysia/Thailand border. I am not sure I can today, but in the straits of Malacca I can clearly see the islands of Pulau Pantal, Pulau Bidan, Pulau Telur and Bunting Island all hugging the mainland.

A cruise ship is making its way slowly towards Penang but is still hours away and although I cannot make them out, I can see the wakes of some small boats, probably fishermen now heading back with the day's catch.

The view also serves to remind me of what we don't have time to visit, I wish we had more time on this trip. The northern most province of Kedah which borders Thailand is also clearly visible. I know there is so much more to explore but it will just have to serve to whet our appetites for another trip.

One more landmark I had hoped to see was the second Penang bridge and there, to the southwest, it is faintly visible snaking its way from the south of the island towards the mainland.

Despite being able to drink in new sights at every turn, the heat is so enervating that we also need to drink literally, and we make our way down the track towards the café but are distracted halfway when we come across a giant swing.

It is like a huge swinging chair that one might see

on the veranda in an American Western but it swings outwards from the trees into an open patch of sky and soars over the trees below. Sadly, for us, several people have had the same idea so we do eventually have to concede the swing to those who have waited patiently behind us.

Never mind, there has to be coffee and a little gift shop to come.

The café here is really good. Suitably refreshed, and stuffed with cheesecake, which was not in our original plan, we decide to enjoy the walk back to the temples and the Funicular. There is a courtesy buggy available but there is so much to see from this vantage point and being in no hurry, it seems a shame to miss anything.

Every so often along the path there are small reminders of England. A red post box here, a small garden ornament there, little seats like English park benches, sheltered under tropical flowers and dedicated to the memory of those who tread this path long ago.

It is very quaint and you can almost feel the countless memories that were made by travellers who came here long ago, floating in the air like blossoms on the wind.

When we reach our destination, we pause to look down over Penang and Georgetown. From up here the city looks quite green, but our thoughts turn to days gone by when Lily was growing up here in the 1920s and her visits here to see family during the Japanese occupation in the second world war.

I wonder what a Georgetown of that era might have looked like, with more trees, little motorised traffic, shorn of its skyscrapers and perhaps eighty percent of its current population.

Ironically, because we didn't buy fast track tickets, we now have plenty of time to contemplate the past because the queue to go down the hill is huge and it is not moving very quickly.

To make matters worse there are lots of groups of children here, perhaps school outings despite it being the weekend, but they all seem to have privileged access too.

I don't care, work is eight thousand miles away, its thirty odd degrees and the views are amazing.

KEK LOK SI TEMPLE

Although sitting in the queue for the train for almost an hour wasn't in the plan this morning, staying on Penang Hill until late afternoon was.

Another fabulous sight for any visitor to Georgetown to see is the Kek Lok Si Temple. It surely has to rank first or second on a bucket list visit here; and as luck would have it, it is only a very short drive from the bottom of Penang Hill.

We have plenty of time in Penang so we could have picked a different day to visit the temple but there are so many more things to see here. We don't really want to see it in the daytime again, we have been fortunate enough to do that before.

No, this time we want to see it when it gets dark because, as part of the Chinese New Year celebration, every evening for a month, it is lit up by almost two hundred and fifty thousand lights and lanterns.

In the middle of an energy crisis, courtesy of our Russian friends I won't even try to imagine how much the electricity bill is going to be.

Night time is still a few hours away so we park in the carpark at the edge of the temple complex which seems unusually quiet and then head down the hill past the Kek Lok Si Charitable Hospital to the district of Sungai Air Itam and the rather enticingly named Rambutan Street.

There are rows of red Chinese lanterns above the roads here too, but in the daylight the place looks rather run down. Although there are lots of shop houses and restaurants, I am surprised that almost all are closed. It is late afternoon, perhaps they are waiting for the inevitable rush of tourists after dark, but right now it would not surprise me if I saw tumbleweed blowing across the road and a Malaysian version of the gunfight at the OK Corral unfold.

Further down the street I can see some life and it looks like this very simple little restaurant is the place to be.

The menu isn't what you would call extensive, it's either Assam Laksa with vegetable spring rolls or go hungry. Fortunately, Sue likes Assam Laksa and the idea of vegetable spring rolls is growing me. This is a favourite dish locally, it is part of a type of cooking called Nyonya.

The Laksa is being made here in large metal vats and is served in a soup bowl. The dish itself is basically noodles supplemented with whatever seasonal fresh vegetables are to hand, then cooked in a fish broth. It is then made piquant, sour, and fiery with a mix of added spices, peppers, or chillies to suit the local taste.

Water does not really take the edge off the chillies but fortunately they are also doing a roaring trade in fresh coconuts so if you visit here and don't have a strong constitution for spicy food, take my advice and leave a little room for dessert.

At home we are used to seeing the brown, hairy coconut which is actually the core of what they harvest. The fruit of the coconut here is considerably larger, about the size of a football and they still have the green outer layer of the husk. The tops are roughly cut with a machete and handed over as they are, with a couple of drinking straws and a spoon to allow you to scoop some of the softer flesh out if you are so inclined once you have finished the coconut water inside.

People often think of this as coconut milk but that it not the case. Coconut milk is made from compressing and processing the white flesh inside.

All in all, it is lovely meal for just a few ringgits, but although I don't know it yet something in the mixture has a surprise in store.

By now we are both quite tired, we've toyed with the idea of heading back to the hotel before coming out again later but we are here now so we figure the best course of action is to spend the remaining couple of hours in the temple, the complex is quite large and there is a lot to see so we head back up the hill.

'Kek Lok' is from the Hokkien dialect of Chinese, and literally means 'supreme joy.' Hokkien is a new one on me. Like most people I tend to associate the Chinese language with either Mandarin, which is the official language of China, or Cantonese, which we are more familiar with due to our historic links with Hong Kong.

Hokkien has its origins in Southeast China and is apparently the third most popular dialect. It is the official language of Taiwan and also seems to be the most popular version of Chinese to be spoken across the rest of Southeast Asia.

The history of Buddhism goes back some two and half thousand years so you would be forgiven for thinking that the origins of the temple would be quite ancient. In fact, although there was a small temple nearby previously, the whole of the current complex was built in just forty years from 1890 to 1930.

It is said to have been the inspiration of the abbot Beow Lean, who chose the site on a hill then called 'Crane Mountain' because it faced the sea. Its construction was initially funded by five Chinese businessmen from Penang known as the 'Hakka Tycoons.'

The Temple is the largest Buddhist Temple in Malaysia, in fact it is one of the largest in anywhere in Southeast Asia. It is an important centre of pilgrimage for people from as far afield as Hong Kong, The Philippines, Thailand, Vietnam, and Singapore.

Anyone who has ever visited any religious building of any denomination knows that, despite the religions being quite well endowed financially, they also all tend to be very adept at fund raising, particularly from 'pilgrims.'

This continues today and funds are used for the ongoing development, which is clearly evident from the fact that a lot of building work is still in progress.

Kek Lok Si really is a complex rather than a single temple. It is vast, covering almost thirty acres and the various parts are connected not just by walkways, but there are two funicular style lifts linking the main levels. The entrance fee is only a few ringgits. It is well worth the price anyway, but it also includes the lift fees.

I could write a lot about this place but the easiest description is to concentrate on the three main parts which are the main hall, the pagoda, and the upper pavilion.

The main hall was completed first and houses the shrine of Guanyin, set in a recessed area where she is accompanied by several other female goddesses, the Queen of Heaven, the Goddess of the Earth, and Goddess of Childbirth.

Even though there is so much ornate iconography to see here, what really grabs the attention are the four giant Buddhas carved from hardwood. Each is about ten feet tall depicted, seated along with several smaller companions on either side and to their front.

This is quite confusing as Buddhist legends tell of five celestials. Buddhas who it is said, have existed since the beginning of time. Yet here I can see that there are only four.

Vairochana, the great illuminator.

Amtabha, the primary Buddha of pure land.

Aksobhya, the unshakeable one, and

Ratnasambhava, one born of jewels.

Their alcoves are separated by giant prayer wheels that look like concrete pillars but which are impossibly easy to rotate with even the gentlest of pushes.

The fifth, 'Amoghasiddhi' is nowhere to be seen, and I am curious to ask one of the monks but right now I have a different priority.

For several weeks now I have eaten almost nothing that would be familiar to my usual, dairy rich, western diet and my gut microbiome seems to be taking this opportunity to completely reset itself to Asian mode.

The Assam Laksa is beginning to make me fart, and I just can't stop. One of the smaller, pot-bellied statues seems to be laughing at me. Indeed, it is known as the 'laughing Buddha' but in this place, which is sacred to so many people, this is making me really uncomfortable so I head for the pagoda on the middle level of the complex.

The white pagoda is an ornate tower with seven accessible levels that get progressively smaller as you climb up it. Fortunately, at the moment, it has been largely stripped bare for a renovation project which is underway, so there is almost no one inside and, it is also open to the air. Needless to say, the exercise of walking up the steps is doing nothing to help my situation. At the top of the pagoda, I pause to look out over Penang and it is like the heavens are also feeling uncomfortable. The wind there too is starting to blow, and it is bringing some dark clouds in its wake.

Once you have visited the pagoda, you reach the top of

the complex via a second funicular and exit through yet another gift shop, out onto a large, flat split-level area.

On the lower part there are, amongst other things, a large oblong courtyard, a fishpond with a bridge and a small wooden pagoda in the centre. The pool seems to be constantly being refilled from a waterfall flowing down the rock face where the edges of the pond have been built into the hillside.

The access to the pond is via a small garden which has concrete representations of the twelve signs of the Chinese zodiac. The Rat, Ox, Dragon, Rooster, Tiger, Dog, Monkey, Goat, Snake, Pig, Horse, and of course this years' icon, the Rabbit. It is getting busy now and there are lots of small children sitting on the statues, presumably their own sign, and proud parents taking photos for the family albums.

On the upper-level towering over everything there is another pagoda, an octagonal pavilion, open to the elements on all sides, and underneath the cavernous roof structure there is a giant statue of Guanyin, the goddess of Mercy.

The statue was built in 2002 to replace an earlier one which was damaged by fire and it is absolutely huge, standing over one hundred feet tall. At the rear of the pagoda there are three lines of smaller figures of the goddess all of which are eerily lifelike and they are freaking Sue out.

Even without the light show, this place is an awesome spectacle. It is getting dark now, past sunset and the lights are still not on. There has been a steady stream of people arriving over the last hour or so and the whole upper level is now thronging with people. We are lucky to be undercover but the people below us are all looking anxiously up at a brooding black sky and hoping that the few small raindrops do not become a tropical torrent.

We wait another few minutes and then suddenly you can hear a collective intake of breath from the crowd as the evening is transformed and we are suddenly in the middle of a rainbow of colour.

There are of course hundreds of red Chinese lanterns hanging above the open spaces but it seems that every tree, every building, every possible nook and cranny is also covered in lights. If you can imagine your average multi coloured Christmas tree lights, it would be like looking at a thirty-acre forest of rainbow-coloured lights.

It is hard to capture the scale of the spectacle and do it the justice it deserves in either words or photos. Sue always says you can never have enough sparkly lights, but with almost a quarter of a million of them here, I think it would be fair to say that they had a good go at testing that theory.

It's not too late, only about 8pm but it has been another long day. It has been a great day though and, thank goodness we didn't try to go back to the hotel and return after dark. As we retrace this morning's journey in our trusty little red chariot, it seems that every visitor in Georgetown, and no doubt quite a few locals are now on their way to Kek Lok Si, and the roads to the temple are already gridlocked.

CRAIG ILEY

◆ ◆ ◆

BABAS AND NYONYAS

I don't fancy another day in the car today so it's time to think about exploring the city on foot. Neither do I fancy breakfast in the main restaurant which seems to have become very busy at all hours of the day and night.

Fortunately, I have discovered that there is a much smaller dining room on the sixth floor where we can enjoy a much quieter and more leisurely start to the day, seated on the terrace overlooking the sea with only the occasional cheeky crow to disturb us, cawing as it hops along the balcony ledge to take a sip of water from the fountain flowing into the swimming pool beside us.

Being Sunday, it should in theory be a little less hectic. There is a lot to see and we have, amongst other things, promised to look in on St Xavier's, to tell Peter what has become of his old school.

My mind is racing ahead thinking of the things I want to see today and I am also curious to understand how it all got here. What makes this place what it has become?

On the one hand, nature reigns supreme. You can't ignore how she has shaped the land, the seas, and the mountains, but on the other, I don't live in the sea or the mountains and I want to understand how the people have added their own cultural veneer to this place.

The Chinese influence in Malaysia seems to peak in the areas of Penang and Ipoh but here in particular the Peranakan culture really emerges into the light and this is probably a good place to pause and consider in a little more detail, the rich ethnic mix in the country.

The original Malay people are not, in fact, either the majority of the population, nor are they the ones running the country. The government does offer support to the indigenous people for things like education and housing, but this assistance come with a price.

Unfortunately the price of converting to the state religion of Islam and giving up much of their own culture is considered too high a price for many of them. Even here on the mainland, for the most part they, the 'Orang Asli', still live very simply in, or on the edge of, the rain forests and sadly in some respects on the margins of Malay society.

The people we associate with Malaysia today, and the ones who are responsible for the country's religion, state structures etc in fact came from Indonesia around a thousand years ago and it is their descendants who now make up the bulk of the thirty-four million or so people who now call Malaysia home.

Those of ethnic Chinese origin are the next largest group making up about a quarter of the population overall but their distribution is not even throughout the country. This is the reason why in some areas, like Penang, their cultural influence is more prevalent.

There has always been trade and mixing between the peoples of Southeast Asia but the European influence has also played its part. The Dutch, Portuguese, and the British all brought in additional populations from areas which had expertise to help further their commercial aims.

The British probably had the biggest impact in that regard with Indians and Chinese workers brought to the country in large numbers in the 18th and 19th Century. In this part of the country the Chinese workers were particularly valued for their skills in mining and working with Tin, and for their shrewd understanding of commerce.

The next largest continent came from India. Southern India in particular, and literally in every city we have visited there is always a 'Little India' and a multitude of colourful temples to their deities. Although we have yet to find it, it stands to reason that Georgetown will be no exception.

Following Malaysian independence from Great Britain on August 31st, 1957, the state continued to develop over the coming decade or so, including adding Borneo and expelling Singapore. As a young child growing up here, Sue and her siblings were oblivious as most children are. Under the surface, all of the usual tensions one would expect in a such a vibrant cultural melting pot undergoing a significant upheaval were starting to reveal themselves.

Social stresses between the different ethnic populations emerged, eventually coming to a head in 1969. There was widespread rioting, protests, property damage, firefights, but most frightening of all, racially aggravated murders.

He was a man of few words so they were always brief but casting my mind back to conversations with my father-in-law many years ago his summary was the country was restructured to ensure that 'Malays' were put first in terms of their culture and economic needs. This is perhaps understandable but it was a double-edged sword with some unforeseen effects.

The Chinese lost some of their commercial pre-eminence and the education system which had been based on the English language reverted to Malaysian first, with English taught as a foreign language.

This is an entirely understandable desire for the people of Malaysia but when we visited Sue's old school in Batu Gajah twelve years ago the headmaster there told us that he lamented the loss of the focus on English.

"It's not the cultural impact" he told us. "It's the fact that English is considered the international language of business, the basis of many legal systems around the world and most importantly" he had said "The new digital world, based around the Internet is being dominated by the English language."

His lament was not some romantic longing for the long-lost British Empire he had grown up in. No, it was solely because he felt that the children in his care might have been much better off and more engaged with the new world that he could see emerging.

These dates and events are important to our visit because it gives a context to the family upheavals we have come to try to understand.

The ethnic origins described above do not tell the whole story of this place because there are no absolutes and of course when cultures mix, like families, what emerges takes freely from both sides and develops something new. One such example here is the Peranakan culture.

There is a famous house called 'the Peranakan Mansion' not too far away. We head off in what we believe to be the right general direction and soon stumble across Fort Cornwallis which surprisingly is nowhere near our intended target but non the less it is well worth a detour.

According to its website: - *"Fort Cornwallis is named after the Governor-General of Bengal in the late 1700s, Charles Cornwallis. It is one of the most interesting historical landmarks in Georgetown. It is located close to the Esplanade, next to the Queen Victoria Memorial Clock Tower."*

The entrance fee is 40 ringgit which is about £8 for both of us. Looking in through the gateway where the attendant is collecting the money I can't see much inside but he assures us it is interesting. To sweeten the deal, along with the tickets he hands us a complimentary voucher for twenty ringgits to spend on refreshments.

Sure enough once inside, there in pride of place, is a statue in honour of the Governor. Have you ever noticed that whenever there are statues of important people from this era, they are almost invariably holding a scroll, and usually in their right hand? There are lots of hidden meanings in statues.

One of many possible interpretations is that if a scroll is in the left hand it is presumed to have been read and if it is in the right hand, it has not. As Malaysia would have been the far end of the empire at the time the fort was founded, it is possibly a hidden symbol of expansion and exploring new worlds.

It may also have been meant as a more subtle but menacing message to the inhabitants of this land. In the book of Revelation, God is described as having a scroll in his right hand and in this sense its meaning is more one of control and authority.

I am about ready for a cup of coffee so we make our

way towards the various stalls which I can now see have been discreetly set up inside the walls of the fort. Although I am not particularly hungry, I am drawn to one with a sign offering 'Pasembur' food, which the stall owner assures us is a unique type of food here.

Well, it would be rude not to try it so we select a few things that look like onion bhajis, tofu, bean curd and couple of very large king prawns before he gets to work. When I say gets to work, he drops it all in a deep fat fryer for about a minute then serves it with a julienne of cucumber, turnip, and tops is off with a sort of sweet chilli sauce.

It's not the most complicated food I have tried here but like everything else it is super tasty. When I add a couple of bottles of water and trade in our vouchers the net cost is about £1.

I don't currently have a soundtrack playing in my head so rather helpfully 'Take me home country Roads' is playing on the PA system. It all seems rather surreal sitting in the tropical sunshine listening to a mellow Sunday morning soundtrack.

Just to add to the strangeness of the day I receive a message from the irrepressible Mr Gan who is once again checking up on us to making sure that we are still safe and having a good time, bless him.

I wonder what he would make of my driving skills? I say skills, but what I really mean is luck.

After exploring the compound, we resume our search for the Peranakan Mansion and as we walk along the street, I am surprised to see a four-foot monitor lizard emerge from underneath one of the parked cars and stroll across the road in front of us. He seems to be having a lazy Sunday morning too.

As it turns out the mansion that we are looking for is not far away at all. It is just a few hundred yards past the Queen Victoria Memorial clock on Church Street.

Church street is much like any other here, lined with motorcycles and cars parked outside the traditional shop houses, most of which are closed today. Towards the western end there is a small garden courtyard, set back from the street which is the entrance to a Chinese temple. The gates are closed and I can see some oriental models doing a photoshoot in the portico but it is the extraordinary green and white building with teak shuttered windows next door that is really the centre piece here.

This at last is the Peranakan Mansion. It has its own little courtyard on the opposite side of the building to the temple, where the main entrance is situated. Presumably once a place to receive honoured guests, today it provides an area for seating and serving refreshments to more humble visitors.

Perhaps it is a genuine fondness or maybe it just serves the purposes of the day, but Malaysia still seems to have a strong link with Great Britain and there, inside the doorway, is a sign that proudly declares that the mansion hosted the then Prince Charles and his wife Camilla in 2017.

Who or what are the Peranakans?

The Peranakans are also known as Babas and Nyonyas

and they are acculturated Chinese people. Basically, that means that they have been assimilated in to and adopted the culture of their host country whilst bringing their own unique twist to it. It's almost like a metaphor for Penang itself; brought down to a very human level.

There are elements of Chinese, Malay, and even British influence but despite this blending it still has its own distinctive style. They created their own unique subculture including pottery, antiques, language, and there is a distinct type of cuisine here known as Nyonya after the ladies of the Peranakan households.

They are unique to this part of the world with their origins around the strait's settlements particularly Penang, Malacca, and Singapore. They are sometimes referred to simply as the Straits Chinese and they are one side of Sue's cultural origins.

Not all Peranakan people were rich by any means, but the wealthy, like those of any age or culture love to show off their success and here it is no different. Inside the mansion she is instantly captivated. It is indeed a grand affair, Tardis like, being much larger inside than it appears from the street.

Inside the huge entrance hall there is large seat made of tropical hardwood and inlaid with hundreds of pieces of mother of pearl. There are many more similar styled but smaller chairs for visitors to take a break from the relentless heat. The ceiling fans are moving the warm air around making it feel like a hair dryer but here and there electric fans do offer some temporary relief.

There are also ornate lacquered screens, large bowls with miniature trees in the bonsai style, bronze statues that would look more at home in a European country mansion, and behind them all there is a grand sweeping staircase that leads the eye to the upper level and the grand pergola over the atrium that fills the whole place with light. The whole place is a riot of colour.

To the left and right there are more rooms, some filled with Wedgwood pottery, delicate Queen Anne style furniture, display cabinets or tables that could fool you in to thinking that you have just been invited to dinner in an English country cottage.

The main dining room is a complete contrast, a table is set for a dozen guests, brightly decorated in red and yellow, typical of the Chinese style.

At the rear there is a fountain which hides a corridor that leads to the kitchens on one side and to a not so small museum and gift shop on the other.

In the kitchen the models from the photoshoot in the Temple next door were enjoying a break and some food, it seems that they also take guided tours in the Mansion. One of the staff explained to us the origins of the Nyonya cooking and if it wasn't already evident, that the owners of this house lived a rich life in every sense.

Upstairs the wild mixture of themes continues. There are statues of buddhas, of various Chinese deities, jade and gold ornaments mixed with European curiosities. Chinese lanterns, ornate metal works, yellow walls contrasting with green Persian rugs and many more elaborate wooden tables and chairs. It is at the same time intriguing and marvellous to see but it is also too much, it overloads the senses.

Now I understand why I have a multi-coloured ceiling light in my dining room.

It's time for some ice cream and a coconut drink, so I

decide to wait patiently outside whilst Sue heads back into the gift shop to make some colourful purchases, no doubt in order to allow us continue the theme when we get home.

On the way back to our hotel, we stumble across Little India. I make a mental note of the precise location and how to find our way back, but for now it is more pressing to get cleaned up and to head out for dinner. It had not been possible to book a table but we had noticed a really busy restaurant the previous evening on Carnarvon Street called the 'A Taste of Tekshen' and we're keen to try it.

We have been told that if we don't get there early there is almost no chance of getting a table.

FROM THE BORO TO BATU FERRINGHI

My friend Alastair kindly bought our whole walking group a little book for Christmas and I have been reading it most evenings.

It is only a small book but full of wisdom and I have been enjoying it immensely. It extols the benefits of walking; it encourages the reader to slow down and take notice of things. It seems to be very much in tune with our trip and whether it was this; or something I had eaten last night; I was certainly noticing things this morning.

The first thing I noticed was that the day started like a bad trip on acid. I felt as though I had one foot in this world and another in a much stranger, more ethereal realm that I could see out of the corner of my eye but could never quite get a good view of. This was pretty much going to set the scene for the whole day.

I was awake even earlier than usual and I was sweating profusely as I had been dreaming about snakes and being bitten by a raspberry coloured one that was hanging in a tree. Like most people I have a natural aversion to snakes. I am not particularly frightened of them, but I do have a healthy respect for them. I know that dreams are not usually meant to be taken literally and for an hour or so I lay awake wondering what it could mean?

)ored wondering and figured out that
ing to be early for breakfast. The sun
et and it may have been due to the
vivid dreaming but I am feeling quietly philosophical today, I can't help speculating about the dawn and pre-dawn.

I love this little restaurant hideaway on the sixth floor. At 6.30am, eating breakfast with the soundtrack of the waves gently lapping at the shore below it is just magical.

Sue asks; "what are you smiling at?"

"I was just wondering is man really made in the image of God?"

"What?"

"Well, if he is, then I was just thinking perhaps the pre-dawn is when God goes for a wee in the morning and nips back to bed for just another ten minutes before the alarm goes off and he turns on the big light."

She shakes her head, raises a tired eyebrow, and asks the waiter for another pot of tea.

I think she was grateful when I was interrupted from my musing when the peace was shattered by a couple of fighter jets taking off from an airfield near Butterworth. Even from here I could see that as soon as they were airborne, they hit the afterburners and turned Eastwards, over the mountains towards the South China sea.

It's true that we only really know what the press

and governments share with us, but if we believe the rhetoric about China's military build-up in the region, then this seems to be most the likely destination.

Today has a personal significance for us and with what is going on in Ukraine I cannot help but worry about close family members. The world seems to be clamouring for war, here in SE Asia, in Europe, and in the Middle East which once again looks like going up in flames as Israeli and Palestinian tempers flare.

I wonder when will the madness stop and offer up a silent prayer to keep all our own brave service men and women safe, and in honour of those who choose willingly to risk everything to defend us.

On a brighter note, today we are planning to explore beyond Georgetown. There is plenty to see here, but Penang is a big island and most people never see beyond the city so to begin with, we are heading north to the beach resort of Batu Ferringhi.

This will mark the northernmost point of our trip in Malaysia this time. For Sue it is chance to recall distant memories of family holidays. I have also been here before and I recall not been impressed.

I love the more relaxed approach before 'health and safety' stopped people having to think for themselves, but I remember this place as being dangerous for children. On that occasion jet skis and motorboats were running up and down the shore, far too close to the beach for comfort. I wondered if I would feel differently without having children in tow to worry about.

The distance is quite modest, it's only about ten miles,

but the drive takes about half an hour. Like everything here, it is an adventure, you need to navigate the one-way system, joust with other road users, and make it out past the busy suburb of Gurney Street, (which is famous for its shopping malls) before the road becomes quite twisty as it snakes along the coastline.

Out here you start to get a sense of what a tropical paradise this must once have been. Palm trees line the road on the ocean side and we keep getting tantalising glimpses of white sand and the odd fishing boat.

Batu Ferringhi itself is divided between the large chain resort hotels which dominate the shoreline and a much poorer but more diverse area on the inland side of the road. Every now and then there are access points between the hotels allowing us to turn off the main road and make our way down to the beach where the stark contrast continues.

The public facilities are woeful. There are a few huts with signs offering boats trips to nearby 'Monkey beach' or jungle walks and there are some very basic toilets, but on the plus side there is a small amount of free parking which makes it is possible to get right on the beach front.

It's Monday morning and at this time of the day, most of the tourists are still either in bed recovering from the weekend or enjoying a leisurely breakfast. The locals know there is no money to be made yet; so apart from the odd jet ski which seems to have been abandoned at the edge of the surf, the beach is all but empty.

The sand looks like powder but is surprisingly sharp and the sand flies are already starting to emerge. I can't decide if they looking for their first meal of the day, which I am determined is not going to be me, or perhaps they are looking for the sunshine which has yet to make itself seen under a cloudy tropical sky.

Despite everything this is a lovely place when it is like this, not at all reminiscent of my previous visit twelve years ago.

The sand stretches for miles East and West and the sea is calm. I know it is only an illusion because the large hotel buildings are just beyond the eye line, but there are trees all along the beach for miles in each direction which give the impression that they are fighting with the sea for possession of the beach. A natural tug of war between the jungle on one side, set against the lapping waves on the other.

There is a lot more to see today but it's time for a coffee break so we head for the nearby Hard Rock Café hotel and resort.

This is everything the public facilities are not. Clean, refined, air conditioned, has great facilities and it is busy, buzzing with people coming and going. The coffee is great but you can expect to pay resort prices, and it also has its own issues.

I doubt that many of the people who stay in places like this will ever see the authentic Penang, which is a real shame, oh and with the benefit of hindsight, I suspect the Michael Jackson exhibits would be a little less prominent.

If you continue following the road West you reach the town of Kampung Masjid, Teluk Bahang. The small village, with its surrounding settlements here have a bit of a Caribbean vibe, a bit like a poor man's Key West, and we can see the fishing boats out in the bay.

Along with the tour boats, they are lined up along the Teluk Bhag Jetty. Much of the North-western part of the island is a nature reserve with limited access, so the road turns south here and leads to Entopia butterfly farm, which is our next stop.

What could be more evocative of a tropical paradise than the gentle flapping of butterfly wings as these beautifully coloured creatures, the size of your hands, swoop over small waterfalls and ponds brimming with Koi or gently sip the nectar from an orchid.

They are amazing creatures, despite being so delicate and living such fleeting lives they are firmly embedded in folklore and mythology.

Ironically butterflies are also symbols of dreams and maybe it's the heat or intense humidity inside the dome, or maybe it's just the early morning catching up on me but I still feel as though I am in one.

If you continue the journey south from here, once you pass the Teluk Bahang reservoir, the road around the island becomes very twisty as it snakes its way through the rain forest.

Climbing up through the mountains past tropical fruit farms and glamping sites at Kampung Bukit Kecil, (which means 'small hill village') the road splits.

There are plenty of places to stop for refreshments but here in the interior of the island, tourism is not yet as prevalent. This is basically a rural community and the facilities reflect that as once again they become increasingly basic. On the plus side they are well ventilated and offer amazing views.

We take the left-hand fork before passing through Pinang village, and we reach well over two thousand feet before the road begins its long descent.

Suddenly the road in front of us opens up and we can see almost the whole of the Eastern coast of the Island of Penang, from Georgetown in the North to Bayan Lepas in the south and across the straits to the mainland beyond.

It's a lovely drive around the island, well worth spending a few hours getting off the beaten track. The concentration on the twisty roads is tiring though; and by the time we reach the apogee of our journey on the outskirts of Bayan Lapas, where the road starts to head North back to Georgetown I am greatly in need of another break.

There is always something to see and a small brown tourist sign grabs my attention so I pull into a small carpark outside a little temple, pay the attendant a few ringgits then we head off in search of a coffee.

Now the day is getting really weird.

This little temple as it turns out is 'The Snake Temple.' It was constructed around the beginning of the nineteenth century to honour Chor Soo Kong, making it older than the much more elaborate Kek Lok Si Temple.

Also known as Master Qingshui, he was a Buddhist monk who lived during the Song dynasty (960–1279) and many good deeds are credited to him, albeit the signs are not too specific about what they were.

His legacy seems to mainly be connected with miraculously healing the sick; but the thing he is now most remembered for is giving shelter to snakes during a really bad storm. It seems the snakes made themselves at home and have been here ever since.

As you make your way through the complex towards the main shrine, there, in the middle of a small walled garden are a few trees with snakes hanging from the branches. These particular inhabitants are highly poisonous pit vipers.

They are mainly dark green on top, the colour changing gradually to a light green, then yellow underneath. This natural camouflage makes them quite difficult to see in amongst the leaves.

At first glance only one or two are visible and this thought seems to be reinforced by the small birds hopping in and out of the tree seemingly without a care in the world. However, if you guide your attention carefully from branch to branch it soon becomes apparent that there are dozens of them and it makes the hairs stand up on the back of your neck.

I am thinking back to the dream that first awoke me this morning and if they had been raspberry coloured, I might be needing more than a urinal break right now.

Fortunately, the vipers are remarkably calm given the footfall here, and perhaps the scent of incense which pervades the air helps to keep them docile, or perhaps there were just born here and are used to people, but either way it is quite unsettling.

By the time we get back to Georgetown the evening rush hour is well underway but we manage to find our way to Chulia Street. I turn into Love Lane and park next to St Xavier's and we head to the Teksen restaurant again, hopeful of once again beating the crowds.

ST XAVIER'S

I enjoyed a better night's sleep last night, and somehow breakfast on the terrace this morning seems a little more like being back in the real world.

St Xavier's will be our first port of call today. Back in the 1960's when Peter attended here the secondary school was private and largely the preserve of the wealthy locals or the children of the Europeans who worked here.

Peter has been following our trip. I am not quite sure exactly how he is following it as he has neither a laptop nor a smartphone; but never the less we have promised to send some photos home.

St Xavier's Institution is what is called a 'catholic Lasallian school.' Like most religious schools their roots stretch way back into the history of the church and it is thought that they have operated here in Malaysia since 1787.

The present school was named after St Francis Xavier. It was established here in 1852 as an all-boys school. In the 1950 a limited number of girls were admitted of college age, but today there are no boarders and it is now a state-run school catering for both boys and girls. In the local slang, the students from the school are simply known as 'Xaverians' or 'Lasallians.'

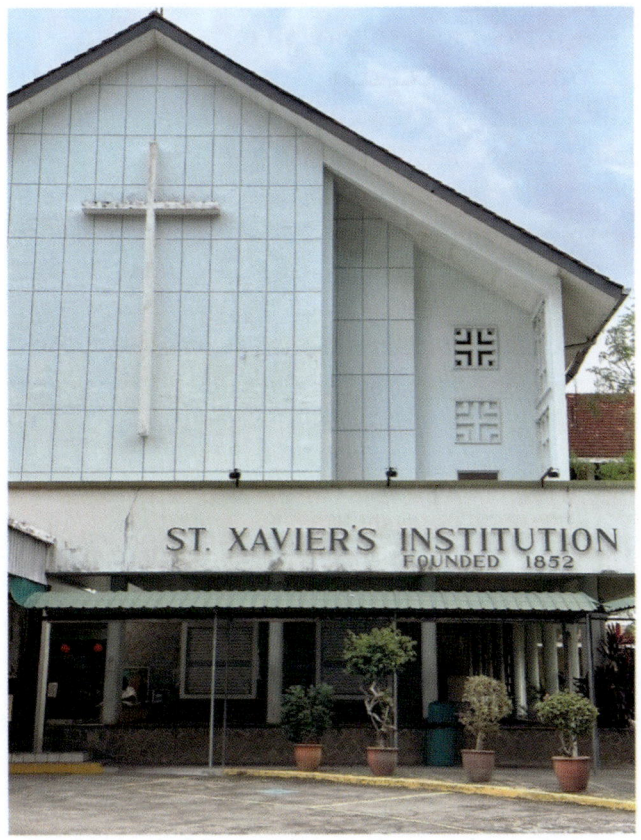

Today the topic of migration is one that very much divides opinion at home, particularly whether people are seeking asylum and genuinely fleeing tyranny, or whether they are simply economic migrants. It seems that although times and places change, people don't change that much.

When people move to new places, they usually bring all their own baggage, prejudices, and problems with them. Here it was the Europeans bringing their religious prejudices to the far-flung corners of empire, and in 1816 the Penang Free school was also established.

This is a protestant school that was setup in direct opposition to the Lasallians as if to remind the far away subjects that the British Sovereign is the head of their church, rather than the Pope.

The more formal entrance to the St Xavier's campus is on Farquhar Street on the west side. It is an elegant cream coloured building with elements of neo classical styling that sits behind ornate iron railings which are topped with the 'Fleur de Lys' and painted white.

Were it not for the tropical plants and the sign that reads 'Kolej Equator', or Equator College, the building itself would sit perfectly at ease in the home counties of England.

Beyond the formal entrance however, architecturally speaking it is not a particularly interesting collection of buildings, which is somewhat ironic as the campus is also now the home of an architectural college.

The campus is more open on the north side and this appears to be the main vehicular entrance. The buildings here are somewhat different. They look like a fairly modern church hall, has been attached to a low-rise block of flats and they look out over a busy motorway.

This is where we had found the only pedestrian bridge over any road that we have seen anywhere in Georgetown. This is seemingly to allow access to the playing fields beyond, which I had erroneously believed were part of the convent on that side of the road.

Along Love Lane on the east side, another block is evident which now seems rather run down. There is also a hard games court which is currently set up for basketball. Facilities like this are a luxury that many British schools do not have, such has been our rush to sell off school playing fields for development in recent years.

I am not sure if it is just me but it all feels distinctly 'odd'. A western game, traditionally played indoors on hard wood floored courts, by people of above average height is being played here, in the East, the home of the best hardwood timber in the world, on a hard, outdoor court, by people whose average height would be expected to exclude them from this game.

When you add in the fact that this is a catholic school but most of the students today are Muslim, and there are speakers around the court which are presumably to broadcast the traditional 'call to prayer,' nothing seems quite as it should be.

In this most mundane of scenes there is hidden, in plain sight, a perfect example of the melting pot that is Malaysia. I can only salute them; they take everything and make it their own.

My overall impression is that it looks like a bit of a haphazard affair today, but this visit is about exploring the past.

Back in the 1960's its location near key establishments such as the Church of the Assumption and the Convent, combined with its large playing fields that still look out over the sea, would have made a powerful statement. It is not hard to imagine that this would have been a very convivial place to study.

At least that seems to be the case when one is viewing it through adult eyes, but perhaps through Peter's eyes as a child it was 'just normal' and at the time he was unaware of the privileges he had.

I wonder what that little boy would think of it today? We have taken the promised pictures to send home; hoping that perhaps they will evoke some memories which in turn might add to our search.

Would Peter remember his travels across the world when he journeyed unaccompanied, enroute to boarding school in England after leaving St. Xavier's, long before the days of direct flights. Would he be able to unpick some of the layers of the mystery we had come here to solve?

For now though, we cannot linger mulling over what may reveal itself later. Time is pressing, we need to make our way through the town towards Armenian Street which is part of the heritage trail here and which will then lead us on to the Clan Jetties.

The Armenian community has also been in Malaysia for at least two hundred years and their influence is also quite strong here. We had come across the Armenian influence in Singapore early on in our journey, with the founders of Raffles Hotel.

As its name suggests, here the vibe is slightly more reminiscent of the Caucasus, with the shop houses converted to ice cream parlours or coffee shops rather than Chinese restaurants. The honey sweetened pastries here are Baklava, Gata or Nazook.

These things are more familiar to us from previous visits to the mediterranean, to Greece or Turkey.

The street is full of the typical mopeds and overhead the rows of Chinese lanterns form ribbons in the sky, but there are also reminders of the British here too.

The once famous British Enfield motor cycle brand is still quite strong here even though the bikes themselves are now made in India.

Somehow, although nothing matches, everything seems to have its place. We had seen the jetties lining the northern edge of the Jelutong highway as we had entered central Georgetown in the rush hour traffic a few days previously.

They looked vaguely interesting as we had passed by them, but then everything does in strange places, and at the time I was more interested in finding the hotel and not hitting any of the other road users. Yet this place would prove to be an important piece of the jigsaw to understanding some of the family's cultural roots.

◆ ◆ ◆

THE CLAN JETTIES

The Clan Jetties have a rather controversial history and if you look them up; there does not even seem to be a consensus as to how many there actually are. Some say six and some say seven.

Physically there are seven but one is not related to a single clan. They are Ong Clan Jetty, Lim Clan Jetty, Chew Clan Jetty, Tan Clan Jetty, Lee Clan Jetty, Yeoh Clan Jetty, and the New Clan Jetty, which is the outlier.

Once there were two more jetties, the Pen Aun Jetty, and the Koay Clan Jetty. They were both demolished in 2006 to make way for some modern flats to be built along the Jelutong Highway which is rather sad as just two years later in 2008, the jetties became a UNESCO world heritage site and they too would been protected.

These very basic communities, with houses built on stilts on the waters' edge, were once the focus of life for the Chinese immigrants who came here for work and trade in the nineteenth century. Given the corrosive nature of salt water it is truly remarkable that they are still standing at all and it is testament to the quality of the local hardwood used in their construction.

Today they all retain their own distinct characters and many of the houses are still occupied. Each jetty has its own temple. Perhaps the most outstanding one is Hean Boo Thean Kuan Yin Temple which seems to be an extension of the Yeoh Jetty, jutting out into the straits. The locals say this is a magical place to watch the sunrise over the mainland, to thank their ancestors or just to give thanks in anticipation of the day ahead.

The best view of this temple is either from the water or another, smaller extension to the main jetty just before you reach the Temple entrance. This precarious wooden walkway, only a few feet wide, is lined with red and yellow banners. They are blowing in the wind and the red and blue dragons seem to be dancing as we walk between them only allowing tantalising glimpses of the temple until we reach the very end.

There are much larger temples here in Penang but this place certainly does have a magical feel to it. The concrete building is painted bright yellow on the lower level, and on the upper level there are two small, elongated structures open to the air.

Rows of red Chinese lanterns line the ceilings and, sitting serenely around the edges of these structures, facing inwards as if to greet their many visitors, are life sized Buddhist statues.

The roofs are covered with layers of terracotta tiles, some are plain but most are glazed in a jade green lacquer; rather cleverly making them look like bamboo branches. Atop each of these structures are two dragons facing one another across what looks like a burning sun. To the rear of the structure is the red brick shrine, again topped with terracotta and jade green tiles.

This shrine seems to be a much more personal affair for the people here. The focus is on their immediate ancestors with the shrine itself containing mainly black and white pictures of parents or grandparents. It seems disrespectful to take photographs inside, it feels more like a cemetery than a temple.

Even though they are happy for us to be here, as some people begin lighting the traditional incense sticks, then wave the smoke towards the pictures and start mouthing their silent prayers, it feels as though somehow, we are intruding on their grief.

The most tourist friendly and probably the most frequented of the jetties today is the Chew Clan Jetty. The entrance to Chew Jetty is directly across from Armenian street and what looks like a market hall, but is in fact another food hall, reminiscent of the hawker centres in Singapore.

All you need to do from there is navigate your way across six lanes of assorted traffic, …. piece of cake. Swivel one of your eyes to the back of your head, stand side by side so that you can look in both lateral directions at once, and finally, when you think you spot the smallest of gaps, run like hell.

The entrance to the Chew Jetty is very ornate, lined with red and yellow lanterns, and you would be forgiven for thinking that this was the entrance to another temple as the roofs of several small pagoda-like structures are just visible set back perhaps a hundred yards from the road.

There is a temple of course, it is just situated a little further into the jetty itself. The path to the jetty is lined with shops and stalls, then before you get to the stilt houses, it opens up into a small square where there are ice cream vendors, hawker stalls, the odd beggar, and a very colourful shrine.

A grey cast iron arch leads onto the jetty proper where the wooden walkway begins, which winds its way down to the water's edge between wooden houses and shops. There are many trinkets available for tourists to buy here, children's toys, ornate ladies lacquered fans, umbrellas, small pot buddhas, dragons and much more.

Once we are in midst of the stilt houses it becomes clear that some families do still live here. The shoes of various sizes piled up outside the front doors are testament to the fact that they are occupied.

We see people ahead of us enter what must be Tardis like properties. They appear to be tiny, like a good-sized garden shed but when we reach them, we cannot see anyone inside. Presumably they are tired of tourists gawping into their homes and they live at the rear away from the boardwalk so that they can get some privacy.

Smoke is rising from some of the huts so presumably there are the stoves on which people are preparing family meals. You cannot help but wonder about the practicalities of day-to-day life here, especially hygiene and waste disposal. To be honest, the plumbing such as I have seen, doesn't look that clever.

Normally this would be enough to freak Sue out but strangely here, walking amongst these wooden huts, with the sea visible between the planks beneath our feet, her gradual reversion to her cultural roots has reached its culmination. Now she is in full Straits Chinese mode.

I am not sure which clan affiliations she feels closest to, she seems to be revelling in all of it.

I am half expecting to hear stories of Auntie Babe, Uncle Kim Seng, and Uncle Yik in an oriental version of Peaky Blinders. I console myself with the thought that at least it would be more colourful than Birmingham would have been in the early part of the twentieth century.

The Jetties are without doubt evocative of a bygone time, of a people living on the edge. Not just literally on the edge of the land, but also at the margins of society and who knows, perhaps of the law too.

It is quite hard to describe them adequately. If you have seen the film Pirates of the Caribbean at World's End, the set which is supposed to be Singapore, where the pirate Captain Sao Feng, (played by Chow Yun Fat) resided, then that would be a pretty good approximation.

If you find yourself in Penang, they are a living museum and most definitely worth the effort to pay them a visit.

When we had first driven into Penang, I was both fascinated, and terrified to note one particular change in the traffic near the entrance to the Jetties.

This was where people started driving their motorcycles, rickshaws, and bicycles in both directions on the same side of the road. The loads they carried also changed. There were fewer pillion passengers, they had been replaced by things like wardrobes, cabinets, huge baskets of food and large gas canisters. I knew that this meant only one thing. We must also be close to, or on the outskirts of Little India.

The heat is taking its toll, now it is time to make our way back to the hotel but this is one thing I can't miss while we are here.

Soon we are standing outside the Hindu Temple on Queen Street amongst the stalls, aromas and colours that have so captured our imagination along our path. It is very busy today as there is festival called Pongal in full swing.

The place is bouncing, the music of the cymbals, drums and high-pitched reed instruments is wafting through the air, where it mixes with the songs and chanting of priests, as well as the unfamiliar voices of the crowd speaking who knows how many dialects and languages.

Lines of worshippers are streaming into the temple and emerging a few minutes later, the tell-tale sign of white ash, or powder on their foreheads indicating that they have been blessed. We wonder if we are intruding perhaps by taking photographs, or perhaps we are simply an obstruction to the people trying to make their way up the steps, barefoot.

A stranger approaches us from inside the temple compound. He greets us with a smile, notes the symbols of Lord Murugan around our necks that we acquired in the Batu Caves then he asks "Have you been to India".

I can't help but smile at his question. "No, not yet" I replied.

We now have a brief resume of our activities at the Batu Caves memorised and ready to go on cue. We explain briefly and perhaps our enthusiasm for the sights we have seen shone through. To our surprise, far from chiding us or asking us to move us along, he invites us to come inside to see what is going on. Then he invites us to stay for lunch in the makeshift canteen that has been set up next to the temple.

The atmosphere is almost carnival like but without any hint of aggression or any edge to it as you may expect at home.

Despite the crowds, this being a strange place and the rituals which are played out in front of us being unfamiliar, even we can almost feel the goodwill and friendliness in the air. The stranger explains that the food is all vegetarian but all are welcome to partake and I can see that the queue is getting longer by the second.

What a magical experience it has been. He can clearly see how impressed we are. Then he drops the bombshell, that this is only a 'warm up' for the main festival called Thaipusam, which is due to take place here in a few days' time. This is the largest festival of the year, it takes place at the time of the full moon when they will take their deities from the temple, parading them through the streets in silver and golden carriages.

The festival has quite a few legends associated with it, one of which is that it marks the birthday of Murugan, and naturally he takes pride of place in the processions. Penang is expected to host almost one a half million visitors who will throng the streets of Georgetown to witness it.

I now really wish we had a few more days here.

ENGLISH ONLY ENGLISH

JANUARY 31ST, 1926.

It is our last night here tonight, we have another long drive tomorrow so a few quieter hours are called for and we have a table booked for dinner this evening on the terrace to make the most of them.

We haven't really made full use of the extensive facilities at the Eastern & Oriental yet and decided that, after our little journey back in time this morning, we would make sure to come back just after lunch in order to enjoy for a few lazy hours by the pool.

The temperature here is so comfortable that it is bliss just watching the clouds roll by overhead and the cruise liners coming and going through the straits.

The 'over servicing' of guests takes a little getting used to if I am honest. Every time I head for the toilet a member of staff follows me to offer assistance which is quite puzzling, and fresh towels which is a little more understandable given the heat. They are, however, all very friendly and engaging. Chatting with the staff I finally discover the significance of Tittiwangsa.

I am not sure if I should be happy or disappointed to discover that it's not just a funny name for a hotel after all. It seems that the mountains I can see on the mainland are the Northernmost section of the Tittiwangsa range (oh that's what it means....!). The scale of the mountain range and its height, some peaks rising to over six and a half thousand feet, not only contributes to making the unique climate but it also forms the border with Thailand which is surprisingly close.

Before dinner I need a nap and Sue needs a haircut. Fortunately, the hotel can accommodate both of our requirements as it has its own hairdresser on site.

A couple of hours later I am well rested and Sue is remarkably chilled too. Apparently, the session with the hairdresser was a combined head massage, cut and blow dry all in one all for about a twenty quid. If she had been a week later, she could also have had her nails done at the same time but they are waiting for a new beautician to arrive.

With or without the five-star luxury, the truth is that it has been very easy to relax here. I have just realised, that this is the first time that I have worn either a shirt or trousers since we had afternoon tea in Raffles in Singapore. That already seems like a distant memory.

Sue too is dressed to kill with her new haircut, new dress, and full slap. We both take a last look in the huge mirror that is hanging over the giant roll top bath and nod approvingly.

We won't be posting selfies on Instagram but we do seem to have both scrubbed up quite well, and then it's time to head downstairs to the sixth floor for the formal dinner pantomime.

The waiter shows us to our table and we play our part, carefully perusing the wine list before turning our noses up at the selection on offer and ordering an orange juice and a jug of water. The waiter doesn't seem to mind, after all it is a Muslim country and although they are always happy to help, I doubt he finds much pleasure in serving alcohol.

He just smiles, he has been serving us for nearly a week and already knows we don't drink but everyone here takes a great pride in performing their duties well. It is as much for the other guests to see as to maintain the tradition and that strange colonial aura that pervades the whole building.

From the balcony I watch the clouds roll in, they are dark, threatening rain and yet the rain does not come. A few minutes later, the warm early evening wind whips up, as it has done every evening here, and the clouds miraculously fade away as if they were no more than black smoke. Strange to say but, the wind seems to have a kindness to it, it almost feels like a soft, warm balm is being applied to the whole scene spread out before us.

This is not just our last night here; it is also a special occasion. Lily would have been ninety-seven years old today and whilst is clear from our explorations that the world has changed a lot since then, this is a place she would still find familiar.

Perhaps the view along the waters' edge, where we can now see the huge cruise ships docked at the Penang Cruise terminal situated at the Northeast corner of the island would be different, but the ships masts, Fort Cornwallis, or the sweeping view across the straits to the North and to Butterworth would all have been familiar scenes.

Most of all, the Eastern & Oriental hotel too, would have been a familiar landmark throughout her childhood, and it took on a more personal significance in the early 1950s. Although it was smaller then, it was here, in the grand ballroom that Joe would court Lily during the tea dances that they both loved. We wish her a Happy Birthday, and we toast all of our parents, albeit with a simple glass of water, and give thanks for the time we have, and have had, with them.

After dinner we head down to the older part of the hotel which today is called the Heritage Wing. Although the grandiose theme runs right through the hotel it is perhaps more apparent here.

The separate entrance to this wing is a small courtyard which is currently lined with hired limousines and high-end private cars. Inside the walls are dotted with pictures of a bygone era and mementos of more recent events including one commemorating the visit of Michelle Yeoh no less.

Then there is the elegant Farquhar's bar, replete with a large case of cigars, a huge selection of whiskies and of course the colonial favourite, Gin. What would sundown be in Colonial Penang be without a Gin and Tonic readily to hand?

But it is the grand ballroom that has the most meaning today and the tea dances of the 1940's and 50's, because in a way, all the events that have led us here today could be traced back to this place. What are the odds that all of these past events and everything that has happened since, would have eventually led us back here today?

Unfortunately, there is a sign outside the door in Chinese which I am guessing means that there is another wedding, either in course, or due tomorrow. I try the door; it is open and there is no one inside so we rather furtively slip inside to have a look around.

I don't know why we are sneaking around as we are both dressed for dinner, we are not in combat fatigues or camouflage, so it should be obvious there are no nefarious intentions here. Besides, they are probably watching us on the CCTV at the reception desk anyway. If they did mind, I have no doubt someone would soon let us know.

I am not sure if it is what Sue expected, the tables set out for a wedding hide the floor space but looking around at the architecture and the balconies that line the walls in the hall, it must have been quite a sight with the orchestra playing on the stage and courting couples whirling around the room in sync with the rhythm.

Having lingered just long enough to take in the atmosphere, imagine the scene, the sights and the sounds from long ago and burn them into our memories, we offer our best wishes to the happy couple who will begin their life's journey together here tomorrow. Then we head to one of the hotel shops to buy some souvenirs of our visit here.

At the end of the day, sitting on the balcony of our hotel room sipping tea, we gather our thoughts about what we have experienced here and ask whether we have found what we were looking for, that elusive link to the past.

I wonder what Lily and Joe were thinking about when they danced the night away here. What plans they had for how their future would unfold together in a world that must have seemed so full of hope and promise after the end of the recent horrors of the second world war.

I wonder too if they sensed the wind of change blowing through their world. We all have our lives, our hopes, our dreams, but we too are all just like leaves floating on the surface of the ocean, buffeted by the winds and tides of events that unfold around us. I wonder what they would think of Penang today and of our journey into the past to retrace some of their steps, if only for a short while.

We must leave in a few short hours, but Georgetown is not quite done with us yet and we are surprised by a huge firework display erupting over the Gurney Street Plaza to the West. Do you believe in coincidences? I don't. To me it seems as if Lily, Joe, and even Penang itself, have celebrated our voyage of discovery here on the island.

What a day it has been, in a few short hours, in the space of probably no more than a mile as the crow flies, we have experienced the cultures and historical traditions of Colonial Europe, The Straits Chinese, The Southern Indians, and the Stirland Clan.

IPOH (PART 2)

There are only two critical objectives in mind for us today, everything else is negotiable. The first objective is to collect our washing from the dobi on Chulia Street, and the second is to make our way to Ipoh, which is a few hours away by car.

It turns out it is just as well that we don't have too many important things to do today, because our plans were thrown into disarray at the first hurdle when I realise that I can't open the hotel safe and retrieve our passports.

Fortunately, Rita who is one of the hotel management team, gets on the case and plugging her laptop into the safe she manages to reset the combination to give us access. Naturally she must make sure that the belongings inside are indeed ours, and that we are not just two scallywags who have broken into the room and are trying it on.

For the first time ever, we were grateful to see someone closely scrutinizing our passport photos.

Problem solved we say our goodbyes, check out, promising to return one day, and soon we are once again in our trusty little red chariot, the Proton Saga. The petrol station is near the hotel so it makes sense to fill up here and top up the motorway toll cards as we have a decided to take a different route back to Ipoh. We take a last look around Chulia street, grab the neatly folded pile of washing, then follow the one-way system to allow us to drive up Campbell Street, Lily's childhood home, before heading out on the Jelutong Highway.

The six-lane highway is busy but it is familiar now and all I need to do is avoid the signs for Butterworth. This time we are not using the Penang bridge, instead we are heading further down the coast to the second Penang bridge or to give it its proper name, 'Jambatan Sultan Abdul Halim Muadzam Shah'.

If the first bridge is impressive running more than four miles across the water then this is on another level. We had our first sight of the bridge from Penang Hill a few days earlier and if it was impressive from up there, nothing prepares you for the scale of it once you see it up close.

Probably the most famous low-level bridge in the world is the seven-mile bridge on the road that leads down the Florida Keys to Key West.

If you haven't driven it, you have probably seen it in the movies. It has featured in Mission Impossible, James Bond Licence to Kill, True Lies, The Fast and the Furious to name but a few. It is iconic, it is also a great experience to drive, and as the name suggests, it is seven miles long give or take.

Just to give some context, the second Penang Bridge is over fifteen miles long running ten miles over the straits and a further five miles over the mangroves and wetland areas that stretch along the mainland coast a few miles to the south of Butterworth. It is so long that it was deliberately designed to snake across the water to make sure that the drivers would concentrate on the road without falling asleep.

This is not just a simple gimmick. It is quite a hypnotic journey as you glide over the water and the rumble of the road beneath the tyres starts to feel like a metronome keeping time.

About halfway across the bridge, out in the channel off to the left, I can see the small islands of Pulau Gedung and Pulau Aman. Unfortunately, we had no time but I would like to have taken a boat trip to visit these islands. They are famous for their giant mantis prawns, which grow to about twelve inches in length. Perhaps I am being greedy, there has been no shortage of culinary delights, but this is one experience that I intend to add to the list for next time.

Eventually we reach the mainland, passing through the tolls and say our final, silent goodbye to Penang. The bridge leads directly to the AH2 main toll road to Ipoh and once we join the line of traffic heading south the journey is straightforward.

It is mostly uneventful until we hit some road works and the traffic builds.

I can't see the trouble but the cones laid out are herding the traffic into one lane and eventually we get to narrowest point where I cannot help but laugh. There, in full road workers uniform, is a plastic scarecrow figure waving his arms like the porcelain Chinese cats that are so beloved here and that Sue is still pestering me to buy.

Eventually the fields and Palm plantations begin to recede; the hills seem to get nearer and once again the luxuriant rain forest starts to dominate the landscape on either side of the road. As we start to climb, it is apparent we are nearing our destination. No, it's not the sat nav telling us. There is a clue in the huge sign on the hillside which proudly says 'IPOH' in white letters that must each be twenty feet high. The approach to the town from the North is stunning.

Ipoh is known amongst other things as the gateway to the Highlands which gives a clue as to the terrain here. It is actually the capital city of the state of Perak and the fourth largest city in Malaysia with a population of over eight hundred and fifty thousand people so it is not surprising that the traffic can be quite intense.

My previous suspicions about the sat nav are reinforced when we reach the outskirts of Ipoh and it starts taking us around in circles as we search for the Wiel Hotel.

We are not too late, it is only about 2pm but soon it becomes a battle of wills between Google maps on our phones, the sat nav in the car, and two sets of eyes scanning the horizon, quite literally hoping for a sign. It takes about half an hour but eventually we see the red brick coloured high rise hotel at the top of a hill, next to a relatively new shopping centre, overlooking the town below.

We are grateful to park up and get checked in as we are both hungry but that isn't the main concern. We were already facing a time constraint in Ipoh. We had made a mistake with the consecutive booking dates for some of the locations and the only way we could get back on track would be to restrict our stay here to a single night. By any standards this would be a flying visit to what is quite a large city.

Ipoh is quite famous for Dim Sum and is referred to by the locals as 'Dim Sum City' and even has a street named after it. Sue loves Dim Sum but I am not keen so I offer to go for a walk and meet her somewhere later. We chat about it for a while but eventually decide that I do like Dim Sum after all, in fact it is one of my favourites, and I would be very silly to miss out on it so now that we are back on the same page we head out in search of the famous street.

Unfortunately, it is quite late in the afternoon now and a lot of people seem to be having a day off today for some reason.

I am not sure why as it's the middle of the week. Anyway, to cut a long story short, when we eventually find it, Dim Sum Street is closed. As you would expect, I am gutted.

We have no option but to continue our exploration and in China town we go in search of Sambal Ikan Bilis. This is a type of hot chili paste made with anchovies. Sambal Ikan Bilis along with the various other types of Sambal chilli sauce, are to Malaysian cuisine what tomato ketchup is to British food. It was a staple from Sue's youth and we have promised to take some of it home for the family but it has been surprisingly difficult to track down.

Despite having looked for it everywhere, we only found one edible jar in a Chinese supermarket in Singapore. There was one more in Georgetown, but it was out of date by some years so we passed on that one and we can't find it here either. The owner of the Chinese supermarket here explains that it is now less popular in a jar and tends to be cooked from scratch or replaced with a cheaper substitute.

The sky looks full this afternoon, the thunder is starting to rumble and the raindrops begin falling. Fortunately, on the edge of the covered market we find a small restaurant, strangely enough it's called 'Ipoh Dim Sum', oh thank God!

Inside it is not quite what we had expected, it feels less traditional and more like a fast-food outlet. All of the ordering is done via an app. At home this is not unusual particularly since Covid but here it is cutting into one of their most sacred traditions, where literally everything seems to revolve around food. We opt for a set menu and the food was excellent.

It seems that things are changing in Ipoh which is probably just as well. For the average tourist Ipoh is probably not a main destination if they see it at all. It has the same feel as many of the run-down industrial towns in the north of the UK.

That should not be surprising as it was built on mining, although in this case the mining of Tin rather than Coal.

As I come from a similar background, I am interested in seeing how this place has changed and how it is re-inventing itself as it is a challenge our hometown shares. This revelation will almost set the tone for the things we will see on our onward journey until we reach the paradise island of Pangkor Laut.

On one level I suppose it is logical, but on another I find it quite ironic that when looking to create a new future, one which embraces new opportunities, that regeneration almost inevitably begins by looking backwards into the past.

Ipoh does have its gems but you just have to look a little harder for them. The newly created heritage walks, the modern-day marketing through Trip Advisor of the historical and very famous Durbar at FMS restaurant, the regeneration around the grand historical buildings, of the palace, the central mosque, and the law courts are just some examples.

The grand railway station sits opposite the renovated law courts and other white stone colonial buildings which are currently receiving attention. Across the motorway there is a small park at the front of the building which stands proud, glistening white under a red tile roof, set against a dark brooding sky and a backdrop of green forest clad mountains. On the floor there is a multi-pointed star with the word IPOH picked out in gold letters.

The train journey to Penang from here is said to be spectacular so I am expecting to see the station thronging with passengers eagerly awaiting their trains.

Sadly, when you get into the station it is a real

disappointment, the old building which was clearly once a jewel in Ipoh's crown is now little more than a crumbling ruin. The old building is far too big to have been just a simple station and as we take a taxi back to the hotel the driver tells us that it was once also quite a prestigious hotel.

We ask about the prospect of renovation having noted that it is going on elsewhere and he assures us that plans are in place. This is encouraging but when I ask him about timescales, he is rather more sceptical. He shrugs saying, "It could be years."

On this I hope he is wrong.

I think he does too but it worries him that Ipoh has announced plans to become what is known as a 'walkable city' by 2030.

Back at the hotel there is a break in the weather so we take the opportunity to visit the roof where there is a pool and it is possible to get 360-degree views across the city and the mountains that seem to surround it. From this vantage point, the location of this city is simply stunning and it is easy to see how centuries ago it would have been of great strategic importance. You could literally strangle the north of the Malaya peninsular from here, something not lost on the Japanese during World War Two.

They had a major presence here making this a very dangerous time for the locals. Japanese soldiers would go house to house in search of young girls, their parents doing everything they could to conceal them. We already knew that Lily had lived through this terror too, we needed to be respectful knowing full well that we could not just explore the past willy nilly, without taking into account the feelings of people who had lived it. Sadly for us, it came as no surprise to find that many of the older generation are still reluctant to talk about it.

It's not late but the weather forecast does not look good so we are not planning on going into town tonight. Instead, we head to the food court in the adjacent shopping centre for coffee and red velvet cake which is supposed to bring good luck.

Ipoh also boasts its very own distinct type of coffee, Ipoh White Coffee which is made by roasting the coffee beans with Palm oil margarine. If you like your coffee sweet, you are in luck as it is usually served with condensed milk. I am reliably informed that it is delicious but I find it far too sweet for my tastes and I can't drink it.

I am not sure about this coffee and cake bringing good luck, personally I think it is more likely to bring on diabetes or a heart attack but I am willing to go on a little faith, it has not let us down yet.

It's been hot and muggy all day and a real storm has been brewing. The downpour of this afternoon was just an appetizer, and when the heavens open again, they do so with a vengeance. I can hear the rain pounding on the roof outside and the sound echoes around the large open space.

No one is heading outside now. Where there is a glass door or a window, the rain is running down it like a river making it impossible to see through. It is like looking at your washing machine on a full cycle. The best we can hope for is to stay dry and hope that it clears the air for the next few days.

This is not going to stop anytime soon so it makes sense to go back to our room; to pack and prepare for the journey tomorrow, attend to our emails and messages. My parents have also been in our thoughts whilst we have been travelling and it's Dad's birthday today so I call home, then I reply to Mr Gan who is still checking up on us as well as a Chinese friend Yao, who is spending his Chinese New Year in the Louvre in Paris and wants to arrange a catch up when we return.

Jobs done I am now free to spend the rest of the evening soaking in the rather luxurious roll top bath.

THE ROAD TO PANGKOR LAUT

I am genuinely sorry to be leaving Ipoh so soon but there is boat to catch so it's an early breakfast and we are on the road by 7.30am. I am looking for the E5 heading towards Sitiawan on the west coast, but the sat nav is looking for something else altogether. Eventually, after a few u turns, we are on the way towards a familiar name, Batu Gajah, Sue's childhood home.

We are not visiting here today. Our timetable is fixed and we have visited here before. Although the bungalow had long since gone, we took the opportunity then to visit her old school which was quite an emotional experience.

The roads here are an absolute hoot and quite the worst we have seen in Malaysia. It is a positive joy to come across bits of tarmac sprinkled in between the enormous potholes. Road markings come and go but where they do exist, in the space of less than a mile the road goes from three lanes down to one lane, to four lanes and then back to one again.

All the while motorcycle riders seem oblivious to this, often carrying small children, they weave in and out of the traffic from both left and right.

Then even more terrifying, there is the bus in front of me which worryingly is moving over to the left and at the same time signalling that that he, or she, wants to turn right. I am expecting the bus to cut across my lane at any minute taking not just us out, but a whole slew of the road warriors on either side of us who are preventing me from taking any evasive action.

Then as suddenly as the madness began, the cars are all herded together and forced to a full stop at a Police road block.

This is more like a military operation than a civilian check-up. There are at least half a dozen vehicles, some unmarked and they are checking all of the cars quite closely. Seeing that we are in a hire car and are clearly western tourists, they wave us through. Whoever they are looking for is probably going to have a very bad day today but we are just grateful to be back on the road.

Pretty soon the road settles down to just one lane on either side, the traffic thins out a little and the buildings along the side of the road give way to the trees, and the forest gradually thickens until it is so dense you can't tell if it is twenty feet deep or twenty miles.

The nature of the dangers of the road also changes. Here you have to watch out for packs of semi wild dogs, laid on the side of the road and the occasional cow as it emerges from the forest then makes its way lazily across the carriageway.

I can't help noticing the remains of the odd casualty too. At home roadkill would be a rabbit, hedgehog, or the occasional pigeon, not so here. You are more likely to encounter a large dead snake or a six-foot lizard that has been warming itself on the tarmac, or the occasional monkey. Seeing a very large python making its way along the edge of the road I am not surprised that the dogs stick together in packs.

The first town we approach is Seri Iskandar, here the road turns westwards and we stop for a comfort break and a coffee in Starbucks. The coffee takes an age to arrive but the attention to detail is first class with the customer service rituals carried out perfectly and always with a smile.

Starbucks is a modern western incursion and it is tempting to believe that Western influences here are relatively recent, but this in not so. Seri Iskandar is named after the local ruler 'Paduka Seri Sultan Iskandar Shah.'

The name Iskandar, however, is a variant of the name of Alexander, an homage to Alexander the great.

This name is surprisingly common in Malaysia, many rulers have taken it as their own over the centuries. As far as I know, he never made it this far but the descendants of his men and the Persians they conquered may well have. His fame and elements of their culture certainly did. Our world has always been more interconnected than most people imagine.

Enough day dreaming for now, we need to get back on the road.

Although Ipoh has always been considered to be the Tin Capital of Malaysia, many of the mines were actually here and the tell-tale reminders of mining are everywhere. On both sides of the road there are the unmistakeable signs of land remediation, cuttings turned into ponds or lakes, and now used as focal points for new housing estates.

Even the road itself starts to undulate due to the effects of subsidence below the surface as old mine workings collapse and are reclaimed by nature, as all things ultimately are.

Seri Iskandar seems to be doing a good job of reinventing itself in a post mining world. The houses look to be high quality and it is developing itself as a university town. There are lots of relatively new campus buildings here, with a particular focus on engineering and technology.

The traffic is building up noticeably now. As we get closer to Sitiawan we are forced to take a detour off the main highway due to an accident. Weaving our way through the palm plantations and small villages we are grateful to eventually re-join the highway a few miles up the road.

Progress is slow for over an hour and as we crawl along, I notice the small communities strung out along either side the road. The traditional wooden stilt houses that make up these Kampongs, proudly display their homemade wooden signs advertising durian, ice cream, hot meals, and accommodation. These ancient communities alternate with modern concrete blocks offering exactly the same facilities. Their signs however are all lit up in neon.

One thing that is becoming clear is that this highway must indeed be deadly. It's not just the pile up that we have narrowly avoided that leads me to this conclusion, there are footbridges here and there too.

It is a good job we did not take a detour to Batu Gajah as the combined stops and delays have left me feeling a little anxious about missing our transfer to the island so I am relieved to reach the outskirts of Sitiawan.

Although Sitiawan is not our final destination, we must skirt the town towards the coast in order to find Marina Island. This small artificial island was created in 2003 and is linked to the mainland by a short bridge. As its name suggests this is mainly a pleasure island but it is also where we need to check in for the boat transfer that will take us to Pangkor Laut.

Although I have grown quite fond of it, I must admit it is nice to get out of the car, into the airconditioned check in lounge where a smile, a cold flannel and a nice cool drink await. As the passports are checked, our bags are unloaded from the car then taken away. It almost feels like going through an airport or customs check here which I suppose in a way it is. This is in effect the front gate of the hotel as the whole island is a private resort.

The boat service runs several times a day, needs to be booked in advance and you need to check in half an hour before departure.

The parking fee is a nasty shock at thirty ringgits a day and I am gutted that my Tanah Rata bingo cards are not accepted here, but this is our last stop.

It was always meant to be a bit of luxury, time to relax, to take stock before the long journey home next week so I grin and bear it and we make our way down to the jetty where a white speedboat is waiting to whisk us away. The crew offer a helping hand to the boarding travellers and once on-board they issue us with all with life vests.

I can swim quite well but as the guy driving the boat is wearing one, I figure you can't be too careful.

As the boat speeds away from the jetty the breeze is a wonderful relief from the heat and once again, we can relax as we are no longer on anyone's timetable but our own. Our journey first takes us past Pangkor Island, we are headed to its smaller neighbour Pangkor Laut.

The larger island covers about seven square miles and it is where most of the resort staff live. As we skirt around it, we can see the rainforest with the odd shack in between the trees, a few small modern buildings and a very large mosque on the water's edge that indicates the population must be quite large. In fact, the island is home to around twenty-five thousand people.

Pangkor Island has always served as a base for fisherman and merchants but once it was also a refuge for pirates. The Dutch built a fort here in 1874 to protect their tin shipments from the then independent state of Perak before the British eventually took control of the region, signing what was known as the Pangkor Treaty.

Although it is another indication of how much there is to explore here, this is not our destination. We are heading out into the Malacca straits, skirting the south coast of the island as we make our way to Pangkor Laut, it's much smaller neighbour. This island is private, it is a resort island owned by YTL corporation, covers only around three hundred acres in total and for the most part is basically a rain forest.

The journey takes around twenty minutes at high speed and once out on open water we can see that there are many large vessels making their way through the Malacca straits. To the south we can also see the enormous terminal jutting out into the straits from the Manjung Power plant, which is situated about five miles down the mainland coast.

Soon we turn northwards in to the channel that runs between Pangkor Laut and its larger neighbour and we get our first sight of the resort. It is everything you would expect to see in a paradise resort. Small wooden villas built on stilts jutting out into the sea, a long narrow golden beach that runs towards the small harbour for disembarkation, all backed by palm trees and finally the rain forest spreading out up the hill behind, its trees reaching up to a pale blue sky beyond.

PARADISE FOUND

Before completing our check-in on the island, we decide to head off to explore the resort. It is not large, but the facilities are extensive.

It boasts at least three restaurants, several bars, a gym, a library, a spa, tennis courts, as well as a couple of swimming pools overlooking small sandy beaches to the sea beyond. All this for just one hundred and forty villas, plus eight estate houses which are discretely hidden away on the north side of the island.

The swaying palm trees are home to a colony of flying foxes. Despite their name they are actually quite large bats that have a distinctive ginger fur. There are also large black, yellow beaked birds flying around that I initially take to be Toucans; but which are in fact Hornbills.

It is quite a compact resort and it does not take long to explore.

The villa will be ready by now so we head back to the reception. Our wooden villa is not on stilts, it is set up in the hillside amongst the trees offering fabulous views over the resort, across the straits to the neighbouring island. The porter deposits our bags in the villa, ensures that we have everything we need and then spoils the moment completely with a rather ominous security warning.

"Please ensure that whenever you leave the premises that they are secure. Make sure that all the doors and windows are locked."

He can see tell by our sudden change in expression that he has set alarm bells ringing in our heads.

"There is no need to worry Sir. There is no crime here" he explains, "but there are troops of monkeys in the forest. They have very strong hands and are quite sneaky. They are fond of the complimentary snacks that are placed in all the rooms, not to mention whatever they can find in the minibars."

"Aren't we all?" I joked.

He has presumably heard that one before and just nods, then he accepted his tip gratefully and leaves us to unpack.

While I examine our new home, I feel a little pang of pity for the monkeys. There is no malice in them at all, they are really not sneaky little beggars, they have simply adapted very well to the environment that we, people have imposed upon them.

The villa itself is spacious with a large balcony but in need of little TLC. The effects of lockdown with no tourist revenue have made their mark even here. There is also an outdoor bath, which I must confess I am slightly suspicious of as is it is currently teaming with the kind of wildlife that they normally use to get celebrities out of the jungle.

I settle down for a nap on the veranda, listening to the birds, the cicadas, and to the monkeys whooping in the trees and .... something else. Oh yes, a bloke with a leaf blower cleaning away the leaves from the path below. I can't think of anything more pointless in the middle of a rainforest and I am quite tired now so after about ten minutes I find myself ardently wishing he would just 'eff off.'

I catch my thoughts in the moment, realising that this is a bit silly because I am here to relax. I tell myself that I will have plenty of time to sleep later. The truth is that Chris was right all along. I have underestimated the toll recent events have taken on me. Although on the face of it I have been quite chilled, deep down I have still got too much going around in my head. I guess it's going to take a while longer.

There are no long twilights here in the tropics, it takes only a few minutes to go from light to darkness but in that short time the forest behind the villa comes to life as the animals come out to hunt.

The hornbills start swooping low over the villa rooftops heading towards the sea. As the daylight fades, the water in the channel gradually turns from a light emerald green to a blue green, then a dark forest green, darker than the trees on the island in the distance, then to a steely grey and finally to black as the last rays of light disappear.

Although it is possible to simply book bed and breakfast here it seems a little pointless when everywhere you can eat belongs to the resort. We booked a full board package and arranged a table for dinner in the main dining room, overlooking the harbour, out to the flickering lights of the small settlement on the island across the water.

As we head down the wooden walkways to take our place, the monkeys have come out to play. They are not frightened of people, but the nursing mothers are wary enough to keep the little ones behind them, and it is the strangest feeling. As if we are the ones in a zoo, and that they have all gathered to watch feeding time for the humans.

The restaurant buffet is superb. There is every type of food you could wish for with more besides. The first night on a new buffet is always going to be a devastatingly messy affair as we try to sample as much as humanly possible.

Sue finally finds the red bean dessert she remembers from her childhood and has been looking for since we arrived in Singapore. Unfortunately, she's already picked up two others, a chocolate brownie, and a bread-and-butter pudding, so it's beginning to mount up, leaving us needing to take a stroll along the front to walk it off after dinner.

It is beautiful here, looking out over the water, watching the lights flicker here and there on the surface underneath the stilt houses with the odd ripple where the fish are jumping, trying to catch whatever they can to enjoy their own evening meal. There is a heady aroma in the air. I don't recognise the scent but it is faintly reminiscent of jasmine or perhaps honey suckle, and the circle of life is very evident here.

The water enhances the scent of the flowers attracting the insects. The insects attract the fish as well as the small lizards and snakes that abound here, as they gently touch the water. They in their turn arouse the flying fox bats which are soon whirling overhead.

The soundtrack becomes more intense too, the lapping of the waves is now competing with the screeching of the bats, the clicking of the crickets and the cicadas until slowly it reaches a crescendo as they all compete with one another to dominate the soundscape of the night.

We head back for a coffee on the balcony before bed. I sit watching the clouds gathering again over the hills on Pangkor Island across the water then I suddenly realise that I have not seen the stars for almost a month since I left home. When I set out on this journey, I wanted to regain my sense of perspective, and nothing does that like planting your feet firmly on the ground with an infinity of stars shining above you in the blackest night.

I would like to have seen the stars tonight in particular as a comet is due to visit us for the first time in fifty thousand years. Now there is perspective for you. Whatever my problems are, whether they be real or imagined, who will care by the time this visitor returns again?

Still, I can't help imagining that this would be a spectacular sight when set against this backdrop, but alas it is not to be. I guess I will just have to read a book instead, so once again I delve into Alastair's little philosophical book and hope I am not hallucinating about snakes again in the morning.

When morning comes, we are down early for breakfast, too early it seems and the restaurant is not open yet so we resume our explorations from the previous day and yes, I have my first encounter of the day with a snake. Walking along the boardwalk around the headland to the spa village I nearly stand on something that looks like a thin, four-foot-long greenish ribbon. Hang on a minute, that's not a ribbon, its wriggling.

Fortunately, the snake hasn't warmed up yet so it's quite keen to move to one side where it hides itself under a wooden bench and just pokes it's head out through the wooden slats to see if we have gone yet. I am fairly sure it's the same variety as the pit vipers we had seen hanging in the trees in the snake temple on Penang Island. I thought staying away from the trees might be enough but I also make mental note not to sit on any benches before moving quickly on.

I smile to myself and can't help thinking "I don't know how, but I am sure Alastair is doing this on purpose." Snakes are a symbol of creativity. He always says we are more creative when we are walking. He's right, but it's just a bit too literal here. I am living next door to a jungle full of snakes so I am not reading any more of that bloody book until I get home. I am already on tenterhooks and the day has only just begun.

After breakfast, which is followed by a few leisurely hours by the pool, we jump on the complimentary bus to make our way to the west side of the island to see the famous crescent shaped Emerald Bay.

The resort has its own resident naturalist, who will gladly take you on a walk through the jungle if you like that sort of thing, and don't mind being eaten alive by mosquitoes. They also have an education centre here just a hundred yards or so back from the beach and it is here we find said naturalist, with a name badge that proudly reads 'Einstein'.

Somehow the opportunity never did present itself to establish his real name, which is a shame, but Einstein is perhaps in his twenties. He comes from a place on one of the islands to the East of the Malay peninsula, Sarawak on the island of Borneo, I think. His westernised moniker suits him because he is clearly both very knowledgeable and comfortable in this environment.

I ask him if I could have seen a pit viper earlier and he confirmed that they have identified at least nine different types of snakes living on the island and yes, the pit viper is one of them.

"Don't grab them by the tail" he said, "apart from the King Cobra it is one of the most venomous snakes we have here."

"Don't worry Einstein I won't."

I am genuinely curious as to the difference between a rainforest and a jungle though as both names seem be used interchangeably here. Einstein kindly explains that a jungle always has tropical weather, whereas a rain forest can be situated in either a tropical or temperate zone. So, as we are in a 'tropical' rain forest it is OK to refer to it as either. Interesting but still not enough to make me want to walk through it in the heat of the day and get eaten alive by mosquitoes. I hate those little buggers more than snakes, speaking of which….

Not to be put off by my lack of enthusiasm for a close up in the forest, Einstein brings the nature to us. He has some small animals he has collected that are temporarily living in little plastic tubs. Mostly, they have been found in and around the few buildings here, so he is studying and recording them before returning them to the wild.

From one of the tubs, he produces a small green snake,

about eighteen inches in length. It seems to sense his ease and wriggles calmly, almost playfully, between his fingers and then wraps itself around his wrist.

He offers me the snake but I am keen to know what it is first.

"It's either a harmless grass snake or a baby King Cobra" he says with an impish smile on his face but he is only half joking.

"It's quite hard to tell when they are this small," he adds looking more serious.

"Erm….I will pass thanks."

I know nothing about snakes but even I know that King Cobras are deadly to humans from the minute they hatch, and this one doesn't look like it just hatched today.

"What villa are you in, I can bring some over later if you like" he said.

"Oh, that's ok Einstein, we are actually leaving tonight" I lied, trying to let him down gently.

"THEY'RE GOOD ON A BARBECUE"

Back amongst the wooden walkways to our villa there is more excitement in the trees, as the staff are having to use catapults to harmlessly chase away the troop of monkeys that have congregated on the railings and are harassing some of the female guests as they head down for dinner.

The ones near our villa don't bother us as we pass no more than a couple of feet from them but we are careful to hold tightly on to our belongings and not to hold out our hands.

Unlike the temple monkeys which we happily fed at the Batu Cave complex; these are properly wild animals. I don't think they would cause much damage if they nipped or scratched but I don't fancy a trip to hospital to get a jab for tetanus, rabies or whatever else they may carry.

If left alone they are harmless but some tourists can't seem to help themselves, feeding them or trying to touch them, then freaking out when the monkeys accommodate. They are completely alien to us at home, but it is funny how strangely human they are. I can't make my mind up whether they look more like a guard of honour or a gang of thugs waiting to pounce. They do rather look like they are on their way to a shoplifter's party in Poundland, but we eventually make it safely down to dinner.

To be honest, we probably over did the buffet on the first night, not just the desserts but the whole thing. So in a concerted effort to get back on track, tonight we elect to eat at Uncle Lim's place.

This is a more formal Chinese style restaurant overlooking the bay but I am not getting off to a good start and the scene is making me hungry. I can see the fish are nibbling at the barnacles which are now slightly exposed by the low tide mark on the rocks. The monitor lizards are eating the fish, the flying foxes have started swooping low over the bay and I am staring at a menu wanting everything on it.

It is here that we meet Ong Hend Ley for the first time. Thinking he is the waiter I am about to place our order when he introduces himself explaining that he is in fact not a waiter at all. He is the residential manager and he is keen to ensure that we are having a good time.

"Oh sorry, scratch what I just said, I will wait for the waiter"

Like everyone here, he is both charming and knowledgeable.

He has seen me watching the wildlife. He tells me that his grandfather used to hunt the flying foxes and apparently, they are quite tasty.

"Is it on the menu?" I ask.

Then he smiles again and shrugs pretending it could be if we wanted it. I know he is pulling my leg because they are a protected species here on the island but I also suspect that even in China, the appetite for bat meat has reduced significantly since the outbreak of Covid 19.

He is very proud of his home country and is clearly very conscientious when it comes to his work, making a point of meeting everyone personally. He is a genuinely warm and engaging person to chat with.

He tells us about Pangkor Laut, Emerald Bay and the other facilities. He is curious to know if we have seen the marble plaque that was erected for Colonel Spencer Chapman. When we say that we have seen it, he tells us that we should also look out for another one, this time near the spa village. That one he tells us, was erected in honour of Luciano Pavarotti, who presided over its official opening in September 2002.

Apparently, Pangkor Laut was named the top resort in the world in 2003 and although he is discreet about their identities, he tells us they have hosted many celebrities over the years in the secluded estate properties. I ask if that is what the helicopter landing pad is for that I had noticed just out of sight around the headland; and he nods.

I point to the six-foot monitor lizard on the beach and ask, "is it ok to swim here?"

Again, he just laughs

"Yes of course it is. The lizards won't bother you. Just don't surprise them in the morning when they are trying to warm up on the rocks".

"Why? "I ask.

"They find it difficult to run away when they are cold."

Without breaking stride in the conversation and almost absent mindedly, he adds "good on a barbecue." I assume he means to be eaten rather than invited. I just smile and let it go over my head.

Most people prefer the pools here because the water is often not the bright clear blue that you would expect to see. It is because the waters of the straits are relatively shallow. On the Western side of the island, there can be quite a lot of shipping traffic in the Malacca Straits where it joins the Andaman Sea. The waters he assures us are clean, but along with the rainfall running off from the land, it can result in a fair amount of sediment and sometimes it appears cloudy or more of a milky emerald green.

We tell him that we are sad not to have been able to visit the East side of the Malay peninsula due to the monsoon season and explain the family connection. He agrees that it is a shame; but is adamant that we must come back. They have a sister resort over on the East Coast which he highly recommends and apparently, the waters on the East Coast which borders the South China Sea, are much clearer if you like water sports in general or snorkelling in particular.

As he is talking, I can see a strange looking boat coming around the headland travelling south. It sits quite low in the water and has what looks a square tower right in the centre. I can also just make out two large protruding beams at the rear, each covered with large nets.

A moment later another appears, then another, and finally a fourth. As they get closer it becomes clear that they are sailing in formation through the channel. Although they are obviously working boats, they are very colourful and strangely beautiful in the moonlight.

"That's the Anchovy fleet he explains, there will be more of them and they will be out for the next few days at least. Anchovies are a very important ingredient in Malaysian cuisine."

He glances at his watch then apologises that he has to leave explaining that we may not see him again for a few days. When we enquire why, he explains that his family home is in Alor Setar, a town in northern Kedah near the Thai border. He became a father some months ago to a daughter named Matilda but he has not met her yet, so understandably he is excited to get home.

I can't help thinking that once again, here is the theme of families parted that just seems so normal here. We wish him well and hope that we do meet again.

All in all, dinner at Uncle Lim's was superb rounding off another very interesting day.

"HIS NAME IS KEVIN"

Sunday is a day for chilling and a few hours by the pool for me while Sue heads to the Spa.

It seems a little quieter today and then I remember it is Thaipusam, so some of the Indian staff we are used to seeing around the place are probably trying to participate if they can in some way from their homes across the strait.

The walk to the spa village along the walkways across the water, past the stilted villas is lovely. There is a slight breeze and the sun is out in full force today. It is going to be a beautiful day and the animals seem to sense it too.

The monitor lizards are already warmed up, they are swimming, having launched themselves from the smooth rock platforms they have been basking on, and there are troops of moneys exploring the beaches in the small coves. The little ones seem entranced by everything they touch. One is warily playing with a small crab while its mother looks on, with a look on her face that I can only describe as a weary sense of resignation.

Ong Hend Ley was right, the Anchovy boats are still fishing and I can see them out at sea, they are taking care to avoid the bulk container terminal in the distance as well as the few large vessels presumably waiting in the channel to dock there.

It may seem perhaps to somehow pollute or destroy this vision of paradise, but the bulk container port to the south is not intrusive. It is a long way off and it is only because of its gargantuan size that you can see it all. The truth be told it does not seem to be that busy anyway.

We have been here for three days now and I have seen very little traffic. The structure is quite majestic in its own way and although yes, it is a jarring contrast to the natural beauty of this place. Its giant cranes look like three pyramids on the southern horizon.

As I settle down on the sunbed with a hot black coffee and a cold glass of water, there is a pleasant breeze blowing over the straits and the only sound is the burbling of the water as it runs through the filters on its journey, trickling down into the multitude of streams and pools in this part of the resort.

I have time to read but as I have had enough of snakes, I am not going to tempt fate again so re-affirm my earlier resolution to give Alastair's little walking book a miss.

Fortunately, I have brought other books too. I read widely, although the authors of my favourite books tend to have one thing in common in that they are now long dead, still I can't help but be in awe of them.

I choose one titled 'God Man, The Word Made Flesh' by Dr George W Carey. Like many of his era, long before the invention of social media and mobile phones, great thinkers took time to distil their thoughts, carefully laying them down for readers in future ages that they would never know. What a service they have performed for us.

As I begin to read, magnificent vistas open up in the corridors of my mind. Slowly, I begin to drift and unfortunately, I am soon asleep, baking under a burning sun.

Come lunchtime, Sue is finished in the Spa, which I am reliably informed is fabulous. The only thing left to do now is head to one of the beach bars to enjoy a leisurely lunch.

This is a relief because I am now looking like a boiled lobster, glad to be out of the sun, seeking some refreshment. I guess I am in for an uncomfortable night.

We are minding my own business sitting in the shade at a table in the Beach Club Bar, looking out over the bay, when all hell breaks loose and the kids at the next table start screaming and running away.

One of the Hornbills; that are usually quite happily swooping through the trees just over head, has decided he is hungry and quite fancies a pizza. As it happens one of the kids not only has a pizza but there is also a spare seat next to him, which said Hornbill has now landed on and is waiting patiently to be fed.

I am not sure what all the fuss is about, he seems quite polite, not at all pushy but to be fair, they are quite a large bird and their beaks are incredibly strong. Not something that little fingers want to be near, or any fingers for that matter. The kid was just startled, he fell backwards off his chair when the bird landed but he seems none the worse for the experience. The barman comes over and chases the bird away, settles the children down then comes to take our order for lunch.

I am really curious about the hornbills; they are beautiful birds and he explains that not only are they a breeding colony but that they also all have names.

He points to the one he has just chased outside and says,

"That one is called Kevin."

I can't help myself, I burst laughing leaving him looking a little offended.

"I am sorry but you must be having a laugh" I said.

"No Sir, its true" he assures me.

Kevin, meanwhile, seems to realise that he is the topic of conversation and has returned. This time he has decided to pull up a chair at our table, directly across from me, and he tilts his head from side to side as if listening intently.

Well, this is a first for me, I don't think I have ever met a Hornbill before, let alone one called Kevin. As we don't have any food yet he just stares at the menu for a while then flies off but he is never far away.

The waiter goes on to tell us that they are curious birds. Hornbills live together and die together. They only nest for three months when the female will close herself up inside the nest, leaving just enough of a gap for the male to bring her food. When they pair up, they mate for life and each breeding pair always raise two chicks, one male and one female.

Sadly, when one of the pair dies, the other commits 'hari kari' somehow, but I wasn't sure how they did this. Do they over dose on pizza, burgers, or chips I wondered?

He wasn't specific other than to say they really liked fast food, but they also eat some fruit now and again. It seemed a bit morbid so I didn't want to pursue that line of investigation.

Later that day I did eventually find a board near the tennis courts that was filled with photographs of the birds and they do indeed all have individual names like Alan, Brian, Kevin, Alison, Karen…. you get the idea!

After dinner that evening I want to get back to the villa early to strip down as much as I can and try to calm down my sunburn which by now is very 'angry'.

Sitting on the balcony, I watch a boat arrive. It is time for the shift change and it is bringing the hotel workers back to the resort. It docks below the beautiful full moon that is now rising over the island of Pangkor behind them. They are a little later than usual this evening, but the Thaipusam festival is now over for another year and it is time to return to more mundane matters.

This full moon is called the snow moon reminding me that it is February and that we will be heading back to colder climes at home very soon. My skin would welcome the relief but for now at least, here it is twenty-nine degrees. Then as if in answer to a silent prayer the sky itself seem to come to my aid. The evening breeze picks up, soothing my skin and soon I see flashes of light on the eastern horizon.

At first, I wonder if they are fireworks from Thaipusam, celebrating the birth of Lord Murugan, but soon it is clear that this is lightening. Another full on tropical storm may be coming our way. Each lightening flash highlights the silhouette of the island beyond before being answered by a low rumble of thunder.

The cicadas and crickets in the jungle seem more hushed than usual now but in contrast the flying fox bats in the trees seem more agitated and vocal than ever, as they set out on their nightly hunt.

We only have one more full day tomorrow, perhaps

that will give us just enough time to take stock before we begin the long journey home.

COLONEL WHAT'S HIS NAME?

Although we have every much enjoyed the Malaysia of today, the history of this place has been a constant companion on our journey whether it has been in the form of personal histories, religious histories, or the sad inevitability of conflict.

That is also true here at Emerald Bay, where there is a plaque to the memory of a British commando, Colonel 'Freddy' Spencer Chapman.

A remarkable man, he was stationed in Malaysia during the second world war. He was part of an elite commando unit established to stay behind in areas over run by the Japanese.

He fought a guerrilla campaign in Perak and provided vital intelligence on how the Japanese, being light provisioned, riding only bicycles had managed to outmanoeuvre the British and Indian forces ranged against them.

In 1942 supplies ran out leaving his unit in a difficult situation. He and his men were unable to escape from Malaysia which was by now entirely under Japanese control. They lived in the jungle fighting alongside Chinese Communist Guerrillas, but one by one his men either became casualties of fire fights or they succumbed to disease.

He himself was briefly captured but managed to

escape. Then, incredibly he managed to survive undetected in the jungle here on Pangkor Laut for three years, whilst the island was occupied by the enemy for the whole time.

He eventually escaped from the island in May of 1945 by swimming out to sea where a British submarine picked him up.

Today Emerald Bay seems strangely serene, totally untouched by its past. The bay faces West, towards the setting sun which would be spectacular to see when it is not cloudy, and you can enjoy boat trips here to watch it.

After the sunset cruises leave and the buses return all of the guests to the main resort, another favourite for romantic couples is to enjoy a private dinner on the beach here. Tables and chairs are set up on the beach under a swaying palm tree, each with their own small beach fire in a little brazier. The sand is romantically shaped around them like a heart (not a sand castle); then surrounded by citronella candles.

As lovely as the idea sounds you are very close to the rain forest here and one can imagine that it could go either way. Either the perfect romantic evening for two if you are lucky or if you were unlucky, you would be eaten alive by the mosquitoes, little buggers that they are.

Standing in the shade of the trees on the edge of a calm sea, feeling the soft sand between my toes time makes me stop and I wonder for a moment, if only the trees could only talk, what stories this place could tell.

Although it has not weighed on our thoughts, the dark period of World War Two has featured many times in our travels here, from the memorials in Singapore, to the personal stories of both savagery and bravery. We have also been reminded of a tale that Lily once told her children about a strange, cruel race of men.

Ong Hend Ley had also shared some stories with us

over dinner about the time he had spent working in Tokyo during the lockdown.

We were saddened to learn that some of those old prejudices about other races still seem to burn in the hearts of the older generation of Japanese even after eighty years. Some people had refused even to speak to him when they discovered where he was from. All people are shaped by their experiences to some degree but hatred must be a very heavy burden to carry for so long.

As I had listened to his story, I had looked at Sue and I could see her mind working overtime. As he talked, she was clearly thinking about her mother. Wondering how she must have felt, transplanted to an alien world, never to return to this paradise around us. How much had she sacrificed to give her family what she hoped would be a better life?

Here in Pangkor Laut these things have also not been forgotten, but they have chosen to frame their memories in a different way. In honour of the Colonel, the resort set up 'Chapmans Challenge' which now occurs annually.

The challenge consists of a 3.8km run around the island followed by a 2.4 km run through the rainforest, and a 1km swim. Fortunately for the contestants the today the challenge does not end on a submarine, it ends back in Emerald Bay at a beach bar which proudly bears his name.

Thankfully we live in different times. I can't help smiling at the irony that people have been paying a fortune to come here for decades and he had to swim out to a submarine to get off the island. If he were here today, I wonder if he would want to leave…. I know I don't.

Then my thoughts bring me back to our search here. I realise that we can be in the very same place, in the same forest or on the same beach, standing under the same sky, but what a difference the accident of the date of our births makes to the life we are destined to live, to the experiences we are meant to have here.

In the years to come, who will follow in our footsteps, what will they think of us and of our time here?

I also can't help but reflect on Colonel Spencer Chapman's observation that the jungle is neither friend, nor foe. It can be either to anyone. It is the way we look at it that is most important. For the Japanese, it was a deadly place, hiding their foe, but to him it was his larder, his protector, and his salvation, providing everything he needed.

So it is in life, and perhaps I should view the challenges I am facing in a different light, more akin to lessons to be learned than problems to be solved.

After everything we have seen, the places we have visited, the things we have learned about the culture and the history of these places and people, the upheaval of independence, of race riots and the changing world, it was starting to make sense as to why Lily had insisted of her children 'English, only English.'

She had seen discrimination first hand and upheaval. She witnessed girls being discriminated against in ways that in modern Britain seem almost unimaginable. As any good parent would do, she did her best to make sure that her own children would never experience those things.

Through the eyes of today, I find this a great shame, I actually lament what my family have lost. How wonderful it would have been to have my own children grow up speaking three languages without a second thought. How much richer their world, and ours might have been?

It reminded me again of our shared thoughts before setting out on this journey of exploration, of the way we view our parents, and it makes me wonder how we, in turn, will be viewed as parents when our race is finally run.

Parents make the best decisions they can on the basis of their experience, with the information available at the time. We do the things we do, only with the best of intentions but never really know for sure if it is right or wrong. Yes, we are flawed but, if we are lucky, loved none the less for it.

Nothing lasts forever, finally it is time to leave. I take a last look out across the water, the morning mist is rising from the rainforest on Pangkor Island across the small strait and the clouds above bring the threat of rain. I guess the world is just telling me, you will just have to wait to see what comes.

FINAL WORDS

It would be impossible to record everything we have seen and experienced in these few pages but we have loved every minute of our journey here having been welcomed unconditionally by everyone we have met.

They are the ones who have made this journey special. Their curiosity about us and our reasons for being here, along with their willingness to share their own stories has brought our quest to life in completely unexpected ways. They have led us down previously unconsidered paths of exploration, leaving us richer in the process.

It has been a real adventure of exploration in every sense of the word, geographically, historically, culturally, and gastronomically. Surely two of the most rewarding things one can do in life are to travel and to learn. Malaysia, this overlooked corner of Southeast Asia, this tropical paradise, has given us freely more opportunities for both of these things than we could have ever imagined just a month earlier.

Despite returning to the UK with our eyes full of sights, our nostrils full of new aromas, our ears still ringing with the chants of monks and pilgrims, and our minds filled with new memories, we know that we have only just scratched the surface, that there is so much more to see, so we are already planning our next trip.

Did we find what we were looking for?

It is truly humbling to realise now how many people we never knew, and how events in places far away, have touched our own lives. What incredible odds have to be overcome for each of us just to be where we are today.

Our journey has made me realise that we are all part of something so much larger. There are no individual lives, we are all part of other people's stories, just as they are a part of ours.

I can see a vision of peace, not quite yet within my grasp but like the rosy hue of the pre-dawn it seems like a faithful promise of what may be to come.

I have not felt that way in many years, but Chris was right, a few weeks was never going to be enough. Let's just say that the future looks like an open plain with a horizon full of fresh adventure.

What of Sue? Well she is a little closer to her Chinese heritage and her parents, and we have both come to realise with grateful hearts that what our parents give us, starts even before we are born, and it literally never ends.

THE END....OR IS IT?

ABOUT THE AUTHOR

Craig Iley

Craig was born into a loving family on Good Friday 1964 and is still working through his education in the university of life, mainly at the hands of his wife Sue and their three children.

Brought up in Middlesbrough, he has worked in finance for forty years with some of the word's largest companies both in the UK and Europe. He is the co founder of two UK start up banks and has published several books.

PRAISE FOR AUTHOR

"It has never been more important for us all to understand what banks are, how they work and why our banking system is not fit for purpose. Craig Iley has been involved in the development of two new challenger banks and 'SHAKING THE MONEY TREE' explains how we can develop a new financial covenant, to regain control of our economic destiny."

- MIKE SOUTHON. AUTHOR OF THE INTERNATIONAL BEST SELLING BEERMAT ENTREPRENEUR

BOOKS BY THIS AUTHOR

From The Boro To Bilbao

What's it like to move to a city you have never been to before, in a country where you don't speak the language.

One man's funny, and moving journey through Northern Spain on a voyage of discovery.

Shaking The Money Tree

An insiders' guide to everything that's wrong with the UK Banking system and how to fix it. Written in plain English to help anyone understand the secrets 'they' don't want you to know.

"If you knew how unfair the banking system really was there would a revolution by the morning" - Andrew Jackson US President.

Printed in Great Britain
by Amazon